FAITH, HOPE, AND CHARITY
IN PRIMITIVE RELIGION

THE MACMILLAN COMPANY
NEW YORK · BOSTON · CHICAGO · DALLAS
ATLANTA · SAN FRANCISCO

MACMILLAN & CO., Limited
LONDON · BOMBAY · CALCUTTA
MELBOURNE

THE MACMILLAN COMPANY
OF CANADA, Limited
TORONTO

FAITH, HOPE, AND CHARITY IN PRIMITIVE RELIGION

BY

R. R. MARETT

FELLOW OF THE BRITISH ACADEMY

NEW YORK

THE MACMILLAN COMPANY

1932

SET UP BY BROWN BROTHERS LINOTYPERS
PRINTED IN THE UNITED STATES OF AMERICA
BY THE FERRIS PRINTING COMPANY

TO
PRESIDENT LOWELL OF HARVARD

PREFACE

THESE Lectures were originally given in Boston in the Fall of 1930 under the auspices of the Lowell Institution. They were then amplified and, as Gifford Lectures, were delivered before the University of St. Andrews during the academic year 1931-2. In both cases I could reckon on dealing with a cultivated audience, though one not entirely composed of experts; and so felt justified in trying to steer a middle course between the technical and the popular. Thus, on the one hand, I have passed somewhat lightly over the anthropological details, but, on the other hand, have presumed on a general acquaintance with the principles and language of psychology. It remains only to apologize for the fact that my theological knowledge is *nil,* unless a certain training in philosophy and especially in Greek philosophy can be held to imply an approach in that direction. Finally, I would most sincerely thank both those who appointed me and those who were kind enough to listen to me for an experience which has been for me at once an honour and a pleasure as full as any that have fallen to my lot.

EXETER COLLEGE, OXFORD
Feb. 15, 1932

CONTENTS

FAITH, HOPE, AND CHARITY
IN PRIMITIVE RELIGION

I

THE RELIGIOUS COMPLEX

On the hypothesis that his religion helps the savage to live, the question arises whether such help comes mainly by way of thinking, acting, or feeling. Now the thinking is of poor quality, to judge by primitive mythology. The acting, again, is symbolic, its efficacy being held to depend on the intervention of a higher power manifested only for such as are in the right spiritual condition. Thus it is all-important that feeling should provide the necessary assurance of being in touch with this higher power, which, however, is only by gradual experiment revealed as a power making for righteousness.

WERE I by outlook and training a Christian theologian, my first duty would be to discuss the principle on which I proposed for working purposes to distinguish between natural and revealed religion. One who is simply an anthropologist, however, has no need to raise this question of method. For his concern is primarily—if not solely—with the savage; and it will be generally conceded that, in so far as savages have any religion worthy of the name, this must be classed as belonging wholly to the natural kind. Civilized folk are agreed that revelations are not made to the uncivilized man, however much they may be made on his behalf; nor will they admit the authenticity of his claims to inspiration, though put forward by him in all seriousness. In short, as regards the ultimate source of such faith as is in him, the so-called 'child of nature' is not allowed by his superiors in education to have had any other teacher than himself. Religiously rated he appears as no better than *Terrae filius,* a self-made man. Thus the way is clear for a purely scientific treatment of his religion, since there is no alternative in view of current opinion except to consider it as part of his culture—that is to say, of his total scheme of self-cultivation. Here, then, it will be enough to insist on the intellectual, as apart from the moral, interest of trying to bring all the creeds of mankind into relation with each other. Anthropology as a branch of naturalistic, non-normative Science seeks truth of fact as its immediate object, and makes play as if to satisfy a boundless curiosity regardless of other profit. Nevertheless, in its bearing on human life as a whole, no branch of Science, and least of all the Science of Man, can have any real meaning or value save on the fundamental assumption that further understanding must result in a more comprehensive, and likewise deeper, love.

Seeking, then, no wider angle of vision than that which is common to all the biological sciences, let us proceed without further ado to our special task of studying the religious experience of the savage in its emotional aspect. And first, before we examine particular manifestations, it will be necessary to frame some general notion of the relative importance of the emotional element in primitive religion as compared with other factors.

Now we may safely follow the psychologists in regarding life, and hence the religious life in particular, as a triple function made up of feeling, thinking, and acting. In these lectures, then, let attention be directed chiefly to the feeling. If feeling forms, so to speak, the hinder end of the complete mental process, so much the better for the inquiry, seeing that savagery in its turn is at the hinder end of the complete historical and cultural process. Or, again, if we look at mind and culture, not from the standpoint of their becoming, but rather from that of their present being, both alike display a stratigraphy in which feeling supplies the base—a base notoriously more stable than any portion of the superstructure. Now the twofold object of the anthropologist is to get back and to get down. Proceeding, then, either way or both ways together, we reach feeling, or emotion, as the key to the primitive in every sense.

Further, it is necessary to consider whether it is not on the emotional side of primitive religion that its chief, nay, almost its only, value for mankind must be sought. At this point, however, let us go cautiously. I may be told, not without show of reason, that the anthropologist is not entitled to pronounce on questions of value at all—that he must leave such matters to the philosopher. Nevertheless, the biologi-

cal sciences certainly do make use of the notion of
value in a sense of their own, though from a philo-
sophical point of view it is an inferior sense. They
attribute survival-value, as they term it, to whatever
proves helpful in the struggle for existence, being
content to beg the question whether in any and all
circumstances it is better to live than to die. Con-
formably, then, with such an outlook the anthropologist can seek to evaluate primitive religion as a life-
preserving activity. By life he means this life. If,
for instance, primitive religion led on the whole to
martyrdom, he would be forced to rate its biological
value low, regardless of compensating possibilities
such as might suggest themselves to the philosopher
or theologian. Doubtless such a criterion lacks finality, and, if the anthropologist fails to recognize the
fact, he must be firmly put into his place. As, however, a certain optimism is native to our breed, most
plain men and even, it may be, most philosophers
will welcome the proof, if such be forthcoming, that
religion and survival are not incompatible, but that
on the contrary the one is, even at the stage of savagery, a condition of the other. Thus it is not beyond
our competence, while it is of no small interest, to
raise the question whether the value, in the sense of
the survival-value, of primitive religion consists
largely in its emotional quality and yield.

In order to prove that this is so, let us employ a
method of residues. In the first place, let it be assumed
that primitive man is, somehow and on the whole,

the better for his religion in the sense that it is a biological advantage to him. Later on we shall have fuller opportunity to ask how it helps; but for the moment to postulate that it helps will be enough. Meanwhile it is only fair to recognize that something is being taken for granted. True, the universality of human religion is a fact that leaps to the eye. For all that, *humanum est errare*. There are unhelpful, not to say positively harmful, propensities almost or quite as universal as the religious tendency; and it would be paradoxical to argue that we are any the better for having to stagger along under this pilgrim's burden, this load of original sin. For example, the love of strong drink is almost as natural to man as are fleas to a monkey. Yet will any one undertake to demonstrate that a taste for intoxication, however mild, is a biological asset? The fact is that, biologically speaking, the dominance of the human species has for a long time back been so well assured that, success in the struggle for existence being relative, we have been in a position to pursue the path of survival somewhat haltingly, and not without taking all sorts of liberties by the way. Indeed, apart from the invisible host of the disease germs, the only serious competitor of man has, at any rate latterly, been man himself—or, perhaps one should say, the other man. In this intra-racial form of the struggle for life the human types that manage to outnumber and outlast the rest do so by shedding various weaknesses to which mankind has hitherto been generally subject; and, in the case already mentioned of strong drink, the example set by a leading nation in banning it is sure to spread if that nation is seen to gain in dominance thereby. But to shed religion has surely never helped a people to prosper. Though half-hearted experiments in that direction have occasionally been made, it is not practical politics according to the verdict of history. Certainly as regards the savage, with whom alone we are now concerned, religion is the central fact of his existence, and apart from it it is impossible to conceive of him as existing at all. There may possibly be a danger, in the civilized society, of religion being, as it were, side-tracked by becoming overspecialized; but, under primitive conditions, the few are not capable of refining it up to the point at which the many lose touch with it. So much, then, for what is offered merely by way of preliminary induction in support of the hypothesis that somehow his religion is vitally good for the savage. If we are to prove the proposition more fully, we must go on to explicate this 'somehow'. In other words, out of the possible ways in which this vital good might come, we must find the actual way in which it does come.

Now both for simplicity's sake and because there is good psychological justification for it we can treat these possible ways as three. The good that the savage gets from his religion must come chiefly through feeling or through thinking or through acting; unless indeed there is an exact equivalence between these factors, which is not very likely. Which of the three, then, has on the face of it the weakest claim to be accounted a source of value? Clearly, the thinking, if savagery alone be taken into account. Considered in itself, namely, as a body of ideas more or less reducible to words, savage thought upon matters of religion is for the most part sorry stuff. A civilized mind can get very little meaning out of it. Nor is there reason to suppose that a savage mind gets much more out of it that amounts to meaning in the strict sense; though, of course, the thinking may contribute a little towards a total satisfaction which is very great indeed. The fact is that primitive religion is too spontaneous to stand in need of self-justification by way of thought, or, as it is nowadays the fashion to term it, 'rationalization'. Apologetics are symptomatic of a self-conscious age. Thus on the purely logical side so little is attempted or achieved that Mr. Lévy-Bruhl has some excuse for using the term 'prelogical' to cover all the intellectual processes of uncivilized folk. It is true that he allows us, if we like, to substitute the word 'mystic'. I should myself prefer to do so, and all the more readily because it will serve to bring out my point that the emotional quality of primitive religion is all-in-all. In any kind of mysticism, I take it, feeling prevails over understanding, the barest hint of significance often sufficing so long as the attention is preoccupied with the richness or sheer strength of the affective tone. Now I doubt if religion can ever dispense with mysticism

altogether. 'No mysticism no religion', I would venture to state roundly. Even the driest system of so-
called rational theology devised by civilized man
has mysticism in it or behind it. Seeking as it does to
express the divine nature by means of conceptions
that are confessedly inadequate, it is bound sooner or
later, in Sir Thomas Browne's phrase, to 'lose itself
in an O Altitudo!' One can put the same thing in
another way by saying that the language of religion
is akin rather to poetry than to prose. This description would indeed apply to advanced religion even
as we meet it in its matutinal splendour in the litera-
tures of Israel, India, or Greece. But how many
grains of poetic gold have all the prospectors brought
back from the wilderness of savage mythology? A
few, perhaps, but only a few. The raw material may
be there for a thought-symbolism capable of exciting and sustaining high emotion; but, so far, it has
not been worked up into form.

The savage, indeed, has little sense of his deficiency
in this respect, having another means of self-expression that summons his tireless body to the aid of an
inert mind. Religion pipes to him and he dances.
His is not the tragedy of the minor poet whose inar-
ticulateness dams up the passion of his soul. The
primitive man is articulate after his own fashion. So
far, however, as he achieves form in giving vent to
his feelings, thereby acquiring in like degree self-
mastery and self-direction, he does it in obedience
to an order, not of thoughts and words, but of sounds

and gestures. Rhythm serves him in lieu of reasoning. His moods respond to cadences rather than to judgements. To put it broadly and somewhat figuratively, in primitive ritual the tune counts for a great deal more than the words. It follows that, apart from their musical context, the words in themselves can mean very little. At most they supply a sort of *memoria technica* to the ceremonial movement in which they inhere. Thus they are almost bare of other meaning than their reference to their wordless accompaniment. *Nomina numina.* Their sense consists not in what they say but in what they help to do. Hence all the life is gone out of them the moment that they are divorced from their ritual setting. The verbal formula is not self-contained enough to acquire any richness of ideal content; and thus the creative imagination must fall back on pantomime, intrinsically inferior though it be as a medium of symbolistic expression. One might as well try to extract literature from a glossary as to read a religious significance into the interminable catalogue of savage gods and godlings which the less enlightened of our field-workers so laboriously compile. These have for the most part little more than what might be called incantation-value. They are like the nonsense words of a sailor's chanty, which have no meaning over and above the moving quality imparted by the measure.

It may be objected, however, that this wholesale denial of substantial attributes to the primitive pantheon is too sweeping, since divine personages of various grades, ranging from nature-powers and culture-heroes to fairies and hobgoblins, figure so prominently in myth and story. I may be wrong, but am inclined to lay it down that genuine myth does little to invest these beings with personality; while, though story does far more in this way, it is with negligible effect on religion. Myth, as I would understand the term, always belongs to the esoteric tradition, embodying the whole oral part of the rites that the community deems to be of vital import. But this oral part is so subordinate to the gesticulatory or, as the French anthropologists are fond of calling it, the manual part, that any elaboration which takes place in the form of worship is likely to be in the latter direction. This certainly holds good at the lowest level of cult, as for example in Australia, where, though names of power are in use, prayer is virtually unknown. On the other hand, there invariably coexists with the lore that enters into the real mysteries an exoteric tradition, which indeed is to some extent designedly propagated in order to screen them from the uninitiated, and for the rest gives but a secular version of sacred things so far as it touches on them at all. If we term this 'story' as contrasted with myth, we can easily see that story, being altogether less serious in purpose than myth, gives greater scope to irresponsible play of fancy. Moreover, the human intelligence is made in compartments so logic-tight and idea-proof that what in myth would be out of place, or even shocking, is tolerable in story, and may even lend it its zest—as if the repressions entailed in the stern business of religion were apt to revenge themselves in outbursts of mild blasphemy during moments of relaxation. Indirectly no doubt, and in the very long run, story reacts on myth and, acting as a catalytic, enables religion to assimilate some of the variety and colour that are proper to romance. Primitive religion, however, on the whole is rigoristic. There must be no trifling with the set forms of a ritual process which does not need to be made intelligible so long as it is duly enacted. But perhaps enough has been said to make it plain that the element of outstanding value in the religious experience of the savage is not the thinking.

We come next to acting. Now acting, we have just had reason to note, predominates over thinking in primitive ritual. Religion according to the savage is essentially something that you do. Granting all this, however, one cannot fail to observe that the thing done—the drômenon, as the Greeks said—is not the thing that the worshipper really wants to do, but merely a prefiguration or pretence of it. Considered therefore in itself, it is a nugatory kind of acting, a beating of the air. It makes it no better, but rather worse, if the savage at the moment of action is so immersed in his drama that he confounds appearance with reality, and beats the air with a blow that seems to him to go right home. Sooner or later he is bound to discover that pretending to do something is

not in effect the same as doing it, however much it
may feel like it at the time. Thereupon, representation and realization having been contradistinguished
to the prejudice of the former, rehabilitation becomes
possible only in one of two ways. Either a purely
subjective value will have to be attributed to the
mimic act as a method of relieving the feelings, of
predisposing the will to achieve, and so on; or, if an
objective value is assigned to it, then it might be held
to be the occult cause of an event which on the bare
face of it is caused independently. Needless to say,
the savage is no philosopher to balance such considerations against each other with the aid of an imposing terminology. It is almost subconsciously, that is
to say, blindly, that he reaches a working solution of
the puzzle. As far as one can make out, his faith is
usually robust enough to lead him to assign what we
should call an objective value to his rites. There is
little sign that he expects spiritual rather than physical benefits to result from them. The whole material
world is deemed to be within reach of his imitative
blandishments. If he makes mock rain, he hopes
thereby to bring down real rain from the sky. Nevertheless, we must credit him with the perception,
however vague, that a mechanical effect is being
produced in a non-mechanical way. It is a miracle,
and a miraculous power must be there to account
for it. Sooner or later this wonder-working condition
is generalized as *mana,* or by means of some kindred
notion. Whence, then, comes this *mana;* or, in other

words, how is it to be imparted so that every wish of the heart may be translated into hard fact by ritual action? Primitive theology with its pragmatic outlook finds no problem more pressing or more difficult to solve.

Now of possible solutions the simplest would be to suppose that the *mana* originates and inheres in the rite itself. There is evidence to show that the savage comes very near to this view at times, but I doubt if he ever finds it altogether satisfying. On such a theory the rite would be like one of those objects of the environment which impose themselves on the imagination as being extraordinarily useful, or dangerous, or merely odd. The benignant cow, the majestic lion, the uncanny owl afford examples from among the animals; the plants have their balms, their poisons, their fantastic forms; and so, too, the inorganic world teems with its natural wonders, good, bad, and indifferent. No doubt the savage finally brings all such marvels and portents within the range of his formula and credits them with *mana;* but this simply means, I think, that he comes to class them, with himself, as spell-binders. In his view they are neither more nor less than so many medicine-men, his colleagues or his rivals as the case may be. Thus their analogy does not explain the efficacy of ritual action; on the contrary, the analogy of the rite explains them. For a rite is no natural object, but an artefact. It is an instrument which man has devised for his use, even if it sometimes develops such intrin-

sic power at his instigation that the user is in danger
of becoming a slave to his own machine. The rite,
then, being essentially a mechanism, its *mana* is not
the secret of how it works, but—what is by no means
the same thing—the secret of how to work it. Something of himself is put by man into ritual action
before it can accomplish its prodigious effects.
Mana, in short, is in one aspect the mind that the
religious man puts into his work. It is a well-recog-
nized fact among savages that my rite is of no use
to my neighbour unless, so to speak, I hand him over
the goodwill—a thing which, in Melanesia, for instance, can be done at a price. It is not enough to
hand over the tools, one must communicate the touch.
The virtue, then, is not in the apparatus, but in the
directive energy that operates through it.

There is, however, another aspect in which the
spiritual element underlying and conditioning ritual
action may be envisaged. Granted that rites will not
work apart from a certain grace or goodwill, is man
the one and only source and author of this blessing?
Is 'My will be done' the soul of the affair? Now as
soon as the savage has a clear conception of gods,
he undoubtedly prefers to say that the successful
issue of his acts of worship is due to their favour. In
large measure, however, his conception of such gods
or other beneficent powers is derived directly from
the rites themselves. Gods start, in fact, as no more
than portions of the ritual apparatus, and for a long
time remain somewhat passive agents of the will of

the human operator, who to the end must call if they are to answer. On the other hand, these divine beings, who increase steadily in personality, and in a corresponding will to have their own way, symbolize in concrete shape that conditionality which the religious man comes more and more to feel in his efforts to adjust himself to his universe by means of rites. He has been learning all the while by sad experience that he can put himself right with his world in a material way if and only if he first puts himself right with it in a spiritual way. He projects as it were into his own chosen instrument, the religious rite, a refusal to work for the wrong sort of man. Out of his very ritualism—his tendency to impute an independent value to the rite as such—there comes back to him a demand, as from an independent authority, to seek for *mana* within. From spirit to spirit there comes, or seems to come, the message that ritual action avails nothing except for the valiant and pure heart. Thus, just as thinking was found to be relatively unprolific as a source of value in primitive religion, so acting when considered in itself is seen in its turn to be of not much greater importance.

It remains, then, to assign its due to feeling as by far the most fruitful element in the religious experience of the savage. After all, to feel like winning in the battle of life is always more than half-way to a victory which, in the biological sense, can never be complete. Nay, by the aid of such a feeling man

looks clean past survival, which is at best a matter
of racial interest, and contemplates a life everlasting
as the reward of his individual striving. This
dynamical mood is the crown of religious endeavour
at the primitive level. Neither to know, nor to do,
but to feel that he can do is the deepest aspiration of
the savage. He seeks from cult neither truth nor
works so much as a sense of power. Such at any rate
is my reading of the evidence, though others may
interpret it differently. No one indeed is likely to
lay much stress on the satisfaction derived from religion by the thinking part of the mind at this stage of
its development. *Amor intellectualis Dei* hardly
comes within the range of the uncivilized man.
There exists, however, a widespread, if likewise a
superficial, opinion to the effect that the savage is a
gross person who requires from his religion material
benefits and little or nothing more. Will the experts
who know the facts agree that the savage is a materialist after the hard-headed fashion of modern com-
mercialism? Surely they would call him anything
but that—a spiritualist, a mystic, a man who puts
sentiment before business. Some of his ceremonies
may be occasional, when there is definite crisis to be
met, and the precise nature of the help needed is
plain to all concerned. For the most part, however,
they are periodic, corresponding no doubt in a general way with the seasonal life of the community, but
usually occupying the intervals between the activities devoted to material ends instead of accompany-

ing them during their progress. Thus, however much they may have it as their ultimate purpose to further practical ends, they stand proximately for a release from secular cares, a retreat from the world and its worries. Indeed, since holiday and working day are set apart in the calendar of social events, their underlying motives are bound to be similarly contrasted. The utilitarian function of the working day being plain to all, another function must be found for the holiday and one that spurns mere utility. If the former is good for what it brings, then the latter must be good for what it is. It may be that in the economy of life play is but a preparation for work; but that is not how it feels to the child who rejoices in play for its own sake. So, too, that child of nature, the savage, enjoys his moments of spiritual leisure for their own sake. If they help him to live at other times, it is because they enable him for the time being to feel that he is living well.

Yet this analogy with play must not be pressed— not even if with the psychologists we are inclined to treat it not as mere analogy but rather as a homology. Play, fine art, and religion may for psychological purposes be said to belong to the same family, inasmuch as all are alike recreative forces whereby the soul is enabled as it were to draw the breath needed for the rough and tumble of the vital struggle. But religion is sharply distinguished from play by its high seriousness. This differentia does not perhaps serve so well to mark it off from fine art, which, though in common with play it is primarily a kind of pleasure-seeking, reveals in its more refined forms a sincerity of purpose, a depth of inner meaning, a devotion to its own immanent ideal, which bring it near to the spirit of religion; so that it is not without good reason that we speak, metaphorically, of the 'cult' of beauty. Religion, however, is divided from fine art in its turn by being alone pervaded by what has already been described as the dynamical mood. Though a withdrawal from real life *in esse,* religion retains the sense of being real life *in posse* —real life mastered in advance. Thus religion must always yield a sterner joy than fine art. The appeal of fine art is wholly softening; as if it were the love-making attitude towards a responsive universe—a mood of tender and reciprocated dalliance. Religion, on the other hand, promises a mastery over a real life that consists largely of hard knocks. The knight takes a pride in his armour, yet not without a chastening sense of danger, nay of death itself, ahead.

The truth is that, as we have seen, primitive religion is never so far withdrawn from the hard business of real life as to lose touch with it and so to abandon its practical interest. The occasional rite continues to minister directly to the alleviation of critical situations. Again, the periodic rite, whether it bears on tribal or on purely individual concerns, stands in general relation to some recurrent strain for which custom prescribes a cure by way of a retreat into the sphere of the sacred. Yet religious observances of every kind would seem to have an absorbing quality of appeal that causes the participant to feel that for the moment he lives a life apart, is removed to another world. He is on a plane of existence where he seems to do hard things easily. Of course, he is more or less aware at the time that he is doing them symbolically, not actually. Even so, he now feels that he could do them as never before—that, given his present temper, they are as good as done. Thus he comes to value this all-facilitating temper in and for itself, and makes a habit of resorting to the spiritual plane of his own free will rather than by the sheer threat of the wolf at the door. A religious consciousness is fostered by a process of self-nurture. The symbolism which originally faced outwards, namely, towards the material world, is turned round so that it faces inwards, that is, towards a world of its own. This new plane of experience is one baffling to the intellect because the literal, the language of the senses, no longer suffices; but it is apprehensible to the mind as a whole, since on the side of feeling and will the value of the dynamical mood approves itself directly. Herein, then, lies the truth of religious symbolism—not in what it says, for it speaks darkly, but in what it makes a man feel, namely, that his heart is strong.

Strength, however, even spiritual strength, may be abused. To be of vital assistance to mankind it must have become the firm ally of moral goodness. There is a dangerous kind of exaltation that manifests itself in association with religion throughout its history. To the God-intoxicated man it may seem that henceforth in his omnipotence he can do nothing wrong— *non posse peccare.* Not only kings and priests of high degree with acknowledged pretensions to a sacred character, but men of low station, and with a doubtful past to offset their sudden conversion, have been known to claim complete immunity from human weakness on the supposed guarantee of religion. Who can blame the savage, then, if he, too, finds in religious excitement an opportunity, and at the same time an excuse, for extravagances of every kind? After all, he is engaged on the biggest experiment that mankind has ever attempted, and one of which the end is not yet in sight. In an experiment there is always danger, more especially during its initial stages. It was a savage, not a civilized man, who invented religion, so far as it can be treated, in the anthropological way, as a man-made institution. Just so it was a savage who first made fire; and doubtless he burnt his fingers badly in so doing. Religion is likewise a playing with fire. The religious man is engaged in trying out the properties of an element which warms but also burns and scars. Thanks to the predominance of emotion over reason in it, religious experience is always hot. Gone cold it has gone out. Rationalism can at most serve to temper a flame which it does not light and may easily extinguish.

Now in the remaining lectures of this course we

shall try to examine the elemental stuff of primitive religion by an analytic or piecemeal method. Proceeding in such a way as is appropriate to what after all is a biological, not a chemical, investigation, we shall do our best as it were to vivisect this highly complex form of experience, which, though organic with the rest of our nature, is yet so basic and central as almost to amount to a living thing on its own account. For the moment, however, a synthetic or wholesale view of it must suffice.

The immediate question before us is why this experience, though by hypothesis of vital importance to the savage on the whole, may in part prove a hindrance to him instead of a help. The dynamical mood, while making him feel that he is a superman, apparently does not *ipso facto* cause him to be supermoral, but on the contrary sometimes causes or allows him to be quite the reverse. Does, then, the illusoriness which undoubtedly pertains to the thought-symbols of his religion, so far as they are taken literally, likewise pervade the very core of his experience? Does it extend to the strong feeling of assurance behind the weak and obscure perception of the reasons for it? Not necessarily; even if it could be said in a sense that religious experience is make-believe through and through. For we can make ourselves believe what is true as well as what is untrue. Make-believe is in fact the only method by which belief can be reached, since it is a state of mind which must always in the last resort be self-induced, however much objective fact may clamour for recognition. Now if there is truth at the heart of religious experience it must be moral truth. Intellectual truth is more directly the concern of science and philosophy, and, though theology is part, and perhaps the highest part, of philosophy, it does not in itself amount to religion. Again, beauty, which in its way is a third kind of truth, enters into religion only through the intermediation of fine art.

From a biological point of view, however, moral truth is the most important of the three, because it regulates practice, and practice is the final test of successful living. Is moral truth, then, the peculiar contribution of religion? Doubtless some would argue that it could be established independently by means of an ethics founded on common sense. Indeed, a biologist, who forgot that his working assumptions are subject to philosophic criticism, might easily deem himself capable of drawing up a satisfactory moral code simply in the light of what might be called the vital statistics of the species. Rules of conduct calculated on such a basis would indeed be exceedingly helpful so far as they went, having much the same worth for the prudent man as a set of medical directions on how to keep healthy. But the reinforcement of religion can transform this low-level, cold-blooded kind of morality into a passion—a veritable hunger and thirst—for righteousness. Such a re-orientation of the moral outlook can certainly be caused thus, while it is very improbable that it can be caused otherwise, seeing that the pursuit of knowledge or of beauty, however disinterested, has not so general a bearing, and so cannot exert as wide an influence, on the conduct of life as a whole. Religion only, then it would seem can bring about a moral readjustment which from a psychological point of view might be said to resemble a change to a higher gear. In the traditional language of religion it is a rebirth or again a turning round of the soul to the light, a conversion.

It by no means follows however that because religion is potentially capable of endowing morality with a new and deeper meaning it is always bound to do so in actual practice. Moral regeneration is perhaps of rarer occurrence than one would wish to believe, even when religious development is well advanced. We must beware, then, of expecting too much of primitive religion in this respect. Even if it be agreed that what I have called the dynamical mood is the typical outcome of religion at its earlier stages, and that the mood in question involves a sense of exaltation—of what is sometimes called 'uplift'—one has no business to conclude that the result is a heightened morality. On the contrary, the known facts would lead us to infer rather that the excitement generated by cult is almost unmoral in its initial phase. *Mana* is, as Freud would say, ambivalent. Possessed by it, a man is moved to let himself go whether for better or for worse. He feels himself half-god, half-devil; or, perhaps it would be truer to say, feels himself god and devil by turns, since he has been shaken out of his normal equilibrium and is liable to the most violent fluctuations of impulse. He has yet to learn—and he has got to learn by slow experiment—how to become master of a form of heightened energy which at first can only be said to master him. His problem is how to be passionate and self-controlled at once and together—how to conjoin high tension with manipulation. Religion thus brings to a head what is essentially the vital problem as it confronts man, the sole careerist of the animal kingdom. Born in the mud like the other beasts, man alone refuses to be a stick-in-the-mud. At all costs he must contrive to slough off his primeval sluggishness. So he dances through his life as if he would dance until he drops, finding out, however, on trial that he can develop as it were a second wind by dancing to a measure. Urged on by this supreme discovery man has left all rival species in the lurch, while within the race itself the sleepy peoples go under, the savage being far more inert-minded than the civilized man in every way. We are altogether his superiors in the art of self-stimulation; and, though we have by no means yet succeeded in sorting out the good methods from the bad, we can claim on the whole to know better than he does how to achieve an extreme intensity of life which so far from being prejudicial to its duration is positively favourable thereto. To him, however, must be given full credit for divining the general helpfulness of his religion as a means of raising himself out of his inveterate apathy, even before the particular ways in which benefit could be secured, and risk avoided, were at all clear to his mind. Some instinct told him that he must abandon himself boldly to the dance if he would pick up the rhythm, and so dance on more strongly and more happily than ever.

It looks then as if religion apart from morality was neither good nor bad, but just a neutral force. It is possibly a question of words, however, and, if we do not like to speak of an unmoral kind of religion, we can call the experience denoted by words such as *mana* merely the raw material or protoplasm of religion. Indeed, so far as there could be either a religion or a morality worthy of the name that existed independently of each other, one would be more disposed to grant to such a morality a certain positive worth as against any that could be assigned to such a religion. A common-sense morality even if it amounted to no more than a prudentialism, an enlightened egoism, would make for human well-being as far as it went. But a wholly unmoralized religious enthusiasm might seem at a first glance to be about as useful as an earthquake. But the question of value is not quite so simple as the metaphor suggests. We cannot compare matter in motion with something much more subtle in its nature, namely, mind in motion. A spiritual upheaval may have certain devastating effects and yet by relief of tension bring peace in the end. Further, to be agitated is not necessarily to be upset, given the self-equilibrating power natural to every form of life. Once more, a certain process of unloosening may foster growth in the organism by allowing freer play to the expansive forces. Thus if there is something at the bottom of primitive religion which is almost unmoral, it is not therefore to be reckoned an unwholesome affection, a disease of the soul. Nor, again, should it be rated, if harmless, yet superfluous, a mere by-product of an over-brimming vitality; since there can scarcely be room for such luxuries in the economy of the primitive struggle for emergence. There remains a third possibility, which one is led to adopt by many good reasons. The neutral quality is that of something germinal, undeveloped, undeclared. The promise is there, though latent. The tree of the knowledge of good and evil may as yet be fruitless; but it is in bud.

The central interest of these lectures, then, will be to study the first beginnings of the moralization of religion so far as it depends on those elements of feeling that are evidently so vital to the process. Our anthropological evaluation of primitive religion will take into account mainly the extent to which it furthers morality by stimulating the appropriate emotions; though due weight must likewise be attached to whatever impetus is thus lent to the quest for truth and for beauty. Whether such a scheme of inquiry will answer remains to be seen. I can sympathize with the Irish professor who said that he would reserve his introductory remarks until the end of the course. But a veritable jungle of facts lies before us. So having boldly taken a line, let us discover by actual trial how well it will take us through.

II

HOPE

If religion is taken as an intensified expression of the will to live, a positive hopefulness is seen to be the basic element in it. Such an attitude is characteristic of the ancient savage, who mastered fire, refused to recognize the finality of death, and anticipated the control of the animal kingdom in his spelaeolatric rites. The same moral is to be drawn from the rites of the modern savage, whether rites of participation or of projection. All such rites are not merely magical, but religious, in so far as they are normal developments of the social life, and apply an inward spur to its essential activities.

Is hope or fear the mother-feeling in religion? I am about to declare for hope, but I shall do so against the opinion of the poet Statius, the philosopher Hobbes, the archaeologist Salomon Reinach, and, in fact, a host of authorities who in all ages from one point of view or another have come to see in fear the primal impulse that, so to say, depresses men on to their knees. Nor can it be denied that the supporters of fear have a strong case. Assuming that the function of religion is to restore confidence, they argue that one must have lost confidence before one seeks to regain it. To this it may be answered that there

28

would be no point in trying to regain something that
was really lost. The religious man knows that the
confidence which he is anxious to recover is there all
the time, waiting and asking to be recovered. Religion is essentially concerned with a potency; and
what gives a potency its unique character is the fact
that it must precondition its own actualization. Just
so the precondition of an act of memory is not an
emptiness, but rather a pregnancy, of mind. The
very thrust of the life-process, then, so far as it reveals
itself, however subliminally, in and for human experience may be said to consist in a certain hopefulness—a forwardness of reach. Approaching as we
do the history of religion from the side of anthropology, which is ultimately the side of biology, we
are bound to interpret man's religious activity as a
manifestation of the will to live. Now even from
the limited standpoint of biology, which takes life
as a datum-fact that can be explored to some extent
even though both its whence and its whither are left
out of account, there is an immense potency or pregnancy inherent in the will to live, seeing that it is
essentially a will to survive, to live racially. According to nature's prompting, then, no less than according to the teaching of religion, we die to live on.
Biologically and naturalistically speaking, we may
be but putting off the evil day of racial annihilation;
but even so a forlorn hope must be hopeful, and it is
with an analogous courage, born of a desperate situation, that the animal species struggles for survival

and the religious man sets forth to carry heaven by assault. All high enterprise is accompanied by a certain nervousness—an effect of strain which, so long as it does not reach the pitch of a functional spasm, may be even helpful to the action by inducing caution, and a sense of measure. But such nervousness is incidental only. The theorists who fail to observe that the fear of the God-fearing man is but the accessory feature of a mood founded on the bed-rock of hope have likewise failed to perceive that religion is an epitome, a concentrated version, of life itself, that bold attempt to persist in being and to crown it with well-being.

For a signal example of sheer pluck, consider ancestral man, that ambiguous figure looming on the utmost verge of the prehistoric horizon. It is usually held that, unlike the apes, he came of a line that had somehow avoided all specialization, and in this way, namely as the Jack-of-all-trades of the animal kingdom, became committed to a career of unparalleled adventure. A hand that can be turned to any job and an intelligence no less well hinged—such are the hereditary instruments of general utility that have enabled his descendants to accommodate themselves to all climates, and to render fire, earth, water, and air alike subservient to their whim. The emotional equipment needful for this primeval gentleman of fortune was the pioneer temper. He must hope for the best even while preparing for the worst. A certain Micawberism is essential to the man of en-

terprise. He must be cheerful beyond strict reason
—beyond a cold or even lukewarm estimate of the
opposing hazards. For any hazard is an uncertain
quantity, being halved by heroism, doubled by doubt.
From the start, then, man must have been brave with
a bravery inclining towards bravado; for he was
subject, more than any of his specialized competitors
of other species, to a certain instability in his nervous
organization, and must counteract it by an overstress-
ing of the favoured impulse—a weighting of the dice
such as William James declares to be the very secret
of human freedom.

What man, for instance, is to be acclaimed the
greatest hero of all time? Undoubtedly, the first fire-
maker. The gods might well be jealous of Prometheus, who stole fire from heaven hidden in a reed;
for henceforth man was godlike, sharing the prerogative of the sun, the stars, the lightning. Every
country of the earth ought to set up a statue to Fire-
stick the First, a statue hewn gigantically out of
granite. Up to that decisive moment fire had terror-
ized the whole animal world. Though it warmed
and lighted, it must not be approached; its touch was
agony, its embrace death. As regards the conquest of
earth, air, and water, man had his precursors, nay his
preceptors, in many another species; for, taking into
account his theriolatric tendency—his habit of glor-
ifying the beasts to the point of worship—we may be
sure that he was not above copying their methods in
all directions. But there was absolutely no precedent

for tackling fire. Man himself is the one and only prototype of the fabled salamander. The savage might almost be said to live in the fire, to judge by the way in which he sears and scorches his naked skin. And yet this supreme discovery reaches back right beyond the backward limit of prehistory. Inconceivable ages must have gone to the experimentation that resulted in so difficult a technique; seeing that probably not one of us could either kindle or nurse a flame, given primitive appliances of the simpler kind—any more, let me add, than he could fashion an effective tool of flint—without endless practice, in addition to a dexterity out of the common. Neither practice nor skill, however, would have availed our enterprising ancestor if some streak of daring in his versatile, happy-go-lucky nature had not in the first instance tempted him to violate the great taboo of living creation. Well might he aspire to tame the animals and the plants who had already domesticated the nearest thing to a god in the inorganic world. Fire almost matches mind in its subtlety, purity, and independence of being; so that anthropomorphism was hardly at any time needed to vindicate its claim to divinity. Hestia or Vesta was never more than a faint personification of the sacred hearth-fire itself; while, again, the central fire, the Sun-God, was no Man in the Sun, but the fierce lord of the day in his palpably real presence. Not merely terror, then, but a nascently religious horror of sacrilege, must have waited on those early attempts of the importunate inventor to bottle his genie—to enslave it to a trick of his hand. And yet he had the boldness—one might almost say the impudence—to try. In a spirit of presumption bordering on downright mischief he vexed the monster until he had taken the measure of its devilries and could proceed to exploit them one by one. From the depths of his inmost being—from the bottom of the well, so to say—arose a hope. However subconsciously, he had an inkling of an indefinite benefit outweighing the obvious risk. Let the unknown do its worst, he would follow his luck.

Next in order of observed occurrence comes an even more astonishing triumph of hope over fear on the part of early man. Fire may sting, but the sting of death is far more daunting; for, instead of pricking the hide, it penetrates to the heart and slays. Besides, once dominated, fire could with constant care be managed. Prometheus bound the fire more securely than ever the gods could enchain him. But death is no more an instrument of human science now than it was in pre-glacial times. Our medicine may devise methods of procrastination; but it cannot avert the common doom, nor reconcile us to however well-contrived a euthanasia. Indeed, biology has to acknowledge it as a mystery that the creature spent with generation should meet its fate with such manifest reluctance, as if it would prolong its useless dotage for ever and a day. Although the eldest of the Terrors, death remains timelessly endowed with the vigour of its first youth. Yet, instead of succumbing to a fear so everlasting in its enmity, man for many thousands of years has met it squarely with the aid of a no less everlasting hope. If the time-process threatens to betray him, so much the worse for the time-process. He will be immortal; he will overcome the time-process and see it out. Thus, then, so far as force of will could do it, Neanderthal man, to whom we grudge the name of *Homo sapiens,* achieved a future life. There can be no question, I think, that the experts are right in attributing to him deliberate burials with due provision for a hereafter. It is even noticeable that funeral custom is already beyond its earliest stage. At La Chapelle-aux-Saints, for instance, not only is the grave neatly dug and food laid by conveniently, but a cave too small for habitation has evidently been selected for a purely sepulchral purpose. If there was a time when the dead man was simply left lying by himself within his own cave-home, or when, perhaps, the dying man was prematurely abandoned, we are well past it. Nor need we in any case postulate as a starting-point so cowardly a shrinking from the sight and contagion of death as to drive the others away before at least something was done to administer last comforts—a restful posture, food, a fire and weapons to ward off prowling beasts, and so on. Surely hope endured to the bitter end and at any rate a certain distance beyond it, as soon as ever the decencies of life meant anything for the human stock. We cannot, of course, tell by poring over the bare relics of that distant past what vague ideas accompanied these funerary practices—whether animism, ancestor-worship, a theory of reincarnation, and so forth, were already there, in however rude a shape, to justify what doubtless was at first little more than a collective gesture of defiance—a refusal to accept death's blow without hitting back blindly. There is something very suggestive, however, in the fact that the young man of Le Moustier was buried with his hand near a weapon which is of a type that had become more or less obsolete in his day, and was therefore such as might have come to acquire a purely ceremonial value. So, too, the shells associated with the interments of the succeeding period have been interpreted as amulets designed to help the dead somehow, whether by revitalizing them, or by otherwise bringing them good fortune. If, then, we can put any trust in such uncertain inferences, there prevailed in those remote days a symbolism of the concrete type so well advanced that some sort of passport could be conceived as essential to the welfare of the soul in transit. Here, however, we are less concerned with doctrine than with the underlying emotions from which it takes its colour. What funeral custom may do for a man when once he is dead we cannot tell for sure; but what it does for the survivors most certainly is, as they say in West Africa, to 'kill the fear'. Instead of either eating the corpse or leaving it severely alone—the usual reactions of the mere animal—man, yielding to that feeling of an attachment outlasting death of which a few rare examples are to be gathered from the sub-human world, stood by until his bold make-believe had extracted something warm and vital from the cold clay—something that seemed as undying as the continuous life of one and all, the life of the group. It was no empty fooling that could thus strive to outwit death itself, the prince of bugbears. By his declaration of independence man had called a new world into existence. Escaped from death he was as free as any god; and, god-like or not, it was the making of him as a man to believe himself so by hoping it.

Third in order of time, to go by that mutilated text, the prehistoric record, was the victory of hope over fear which resulted in the subjugation of the beasts. The struggle for victory was of course age-long, and must have been marked by early successes, since there could hardly be a cave-man until the cave-bear had been expropriated, as probably only a fire-maker could do. But we have to pass on to the Late Palaeolithic to find definite proofs that the hunter had learnt to fortify his heart with the help of religion. Now his hunting was no soft job. Early Europe did not provide easy meat in the shape of such mild marsupials as Australia offers to its aboriginals, but was part of that central area of biological competition which produced the toughest and fiercest of the mammals. No modern slayer of big game, without rifle or even bow to assist him, would

be any too happy in such conditions as daily confronted the man who in Aurignacian or Magdalenian
times was out to get, and at the same time not to be, a
dinner. Presumably, however, he had long before
this developed the character of an effective killer—
involving not merely the patient hardihood of one
who plies the gentle art of fishing, but likewise the
grim temper which enables a man to spill hot blood
hot-bloodedly. Among the food-animals on which
he preyed some like the mammoth, the rhinoceros,
or even the bison were more dangerous than others
such as the horse or reindeer; but it may be doubted
whether he palpitated in the presence of the ugliest
customer of them all with any emotion less credit-
able than the pure ardour of the chase. Meanwhile,
as regards his rivals, the larger carnivores, we may
suppose that mutual respect had taught both sides to
observe a truce, whereby man had the day to himself,
so long as he clung to his fireside and left the night
to the other shift.

Nevertheless, though possibly the natural fear of
the beast was in large part overcome, man thereupon
went out of his way to impose an artificial fear upon
himself. So as the better to glorify his hunter's trade,
he must gratuitously invest it with a borrowed mystery. Now the most terrible thing in a cave-dweller's
daily and nightly experience was a yawning mouth
of darkness at his back; that way lay the underworld
—hell. In limestone districts such gloomy and tortuous tunnels honeycomb the hills for miles, and teem

with unfamiliar perils—crossways that bewilder,
stalactites that threaten to pierce the skull, streams
and deep pools that must be swum beneath an arch
that in places dips into the water, and swallow-holes
in the footway that could act as death-traps, as one
may deduce from the huddled remains of many an
unwary beast. It was the maddest of adventures that
led the man of old to arm himself with flickering
torch or feeble lamp of the Eskimo pattern and advance on and on into earth's innermost void—a region
barren of all profit and abominably strange. One
can but suggest at a guess that a cult of the cave-
bear—such as perhaps inspired those Aurignacian
designs at Gargas that look so much like imitations
of the authentic marks imprinted by the beast on the
same cave-walls in the course of sharpening his
claws—may have encouraged a desire to copy the
mighty beast's subterranean retirements and roam-
ings. It is good savage logic that, to acquire the
bear's *mana,* one must play the bear thoroughly. Be
this as it may—whether theriolatry, that is, animal-
worship, lurks in the background or not—something
that can almost be ascribed as a spelaeolatry, or cave-
worship, must have come into being as a consequence
of this intrepid exploration of such hidden and
haunted places. The cave itself had *mana;* so that
a man might borrow its faculty of working wonders
were he but brave enough to go in and fetch it out.
Thus half-a-mile within a mountain, at Niaux in
Ariège, one sees how the shape of the natural rock,

eked out with a little paint, could seem to embody animal forms, surely placed there as a sign for the man who had come all that long and dreadful way to see and to believe. Given the ceremonial quality of these mural paintings—for a certain observance of set form accompanies even the striking naturalism of the earlier efforts—one is led to suspect a priest-hood, a body of spelaeolatric experts, who, interposing themselves as it were between the hunter and his natural business, bade him reflect on its precarious-ness, and by facing his fears outface them.

Now we can never know exactly what ritual prac-tices or beliefs were fostered under such a régime, and analogies drawn from the modern savage are but helpful up to a point. In most cases we seem to have a fairly straightforward representation of a successful kill—as when javelins are depicted with their points cleaving the painted hearts of the animal portraits on the walls, or—more vivid still—when at Montespan the clay image of a bear has plainly been transfixed by repeated thrusts with an actual spear. At Tuc d'Audoubert, however, the conjoined bisons, male and female, would seem to embody a fertility motive, a sort of invitation to be fruitful and mul-tiply. Again, the so-called sorcerer of Les Trois Frères, the impressive reindeer-headed man who even now fills that solemn chamber with his presence —not to mention the various masked figures of other caves in France and Spain—implies some doctrine of a communion between man and beast; a relationship which, though perhaps it was not consciously one-sided, assigns all the taking to man and all the giving to his ally. For our forerunner was so innately ambitious of dominance that, even when apparently offering the hand of fellowship to his competitors, he was sparring for an opening to attack them. His pieties were not so disinterested as they professed to be, or indeed, perhaps, as he honestly believed them to be, so far as he tried to buttress his behaviour with a creed. But, even if his universe was egocentric, we must admire him for his effrontery. Instead of viewing himself dispassionately as a miserable mannikin in the grip of hunger and deadly cold, he magnified his prospects by conjuring up the inordinate hope of a prodigious hunting, when all nature, from the powers of darkness to the beasts themselves, should conspire to befriend him and serve his purpose. At bottom then, it was a sort of justifiable megalomania —an exultation of the spirit due to a growing sense of power and of a destiny to match—that, chastened by attendant fears but never yielding to their sway, lent an impetus to the food-quest, while at the same time creating secondary activities that embellished life instead of merely sustaining it. If man was able to wring from the ice-age not only existence but even some of its amenities, it was thanks to an ingrained hopefulness, and to a religion that could bring it out.

It would be easy to find further illustrations, whether taken from ancient or from modern savagery, of hope as an element in primitive religion;

for on analysis it turns out to be the prevailing tone in religious feeling, in fact, the universal key-note on which the harmonious relations of its other elements are ultimately based. It may be more profitable, however, to pass on to examine what the psychologists are wont to call—perhaps not very appropriately—the 'mechanism' of the process whereby hope is encouraged by religious means. Religion, however, is not really like a machine into which one puts in raw instinct at one end so as to turn out a finished morality at the other. Essentially it is a mode of living. Moreover, it is a mode belonging to that higher grade of living when the directive principle, which throughout is self-determining, is becoming self-conscious. That this advance in self-consciousness is on the whole beneficial to the species may be taken as a biological axiom; the presumption likewise being that it somehow affects the directive principle for the better. In other words, our powers of self-guidance may be supposed to improve if, and in so far as, we can achieve self-knowledge. Yet whether we can ever come to know ourselves completely is highly doubtful. We may pipe all the instincts on deck, but there are stowaways who are not likely to attend the muster. At its best, too, reflection is an indirect method of viewing one's true features; one is merely holding up a mirror. When we try to improve on nature, it is by uncertain inference from an image; and nature is apt to protest that we are making a mistake. Religion, then, as an activity of the self-conscious or reflective type has to content itself with imaging, or symbolically expressing, as best it can, something within and yet beyond consciousness, something not wholly given because at the same time giving, namely, the life-feeling itself, the concentrated thrust of the racial instincts. The other animals just live; but man has superfluous energy enough to say to himself as he lives, 'Here I am living!' and somehow it helps him to live better. By a tortuous effort of mental gymnastics he pats himself on his own back and is greatly cheered.

Now in studying religion as a method of self-expression the first thing to note is that religion can have no significance—no signalling value—until it has come to have social use. Its higher biological function is to promote common action, though it may originally have been merely helpful to the individual as a way of blowing off steam. Man, of course, has been a social, not to say political, animal for such an age that, before prehistory catches its first glimpse of him he must have been able to converse with his group-mates significantly enough, even though with a decided economy of articulate speech. In close company, such as the earliest hordes must have kept, gesture would go a long way towards making intention plain. In the thick of action, indeed, an experienced pack would know what to do without much mutual instruction. At leisure moments, however, as at nightfall with hunting over and bellies full, a mood of comfortable expansiveness might well bring about the institution of the chorus. Now man's mimetic choruses are not to be compared too closely with the so-called howling concerts of the monkeys; for, whereas the monkeys presumably howl about nothing in particular, man has that extra dash of purposive intelligence which always makes him want to express himself about something. When human folk are moved to joke and jig together, they must do it to a measure; and a measure in itself wellnigh amounts to a meaning. Thus, ordered movement in the dance is immediately suggestive of ordered movement in the day's work. Again, different measures convey separate suggestions of their own. Some soothe, others excite; some are melancholy, others merry. Once more, they may recall in various ways the characteristic motions—the leaping, twisting, stamping, galloping—of those beasts which the hunter has observed, and can picture, so minutely. Even if we assume, then, that dancing was rhythmic before it became representative, it is easy to see how it would meet symbolism half-way as soon as the dancers had taken to pretending that what they did was, at least for the time being, something else. From dancing to drama was but a step.

Drama, however, does not necessarily involve religion. It may be no more than a form of amusement—anything, in fact, between child's play and fine art. The Australian native, for instance, distinguishes quite clearly in his mind between sacred drama and the mere corroboree. I have myself attended among the Narrinyeri of the Lower Murray a merrymaking of the latter kind. There was obviously nothing sacred or secret about it; the other sex was present; the white man might look on. After devoting an interminable time to adorning their persons with white paint, the men stepped gaily into the ring. The band promptly struck up—consisting of the women squatting with their opossum rugs stretched tightly across their knees and drumming hard with their fists, to the accompaniment of a loud but apparently wordless droning that reminded one of the bagpipes. In strict response to the pulsations of this rude but most stimulating music the performers postured and swayed monotonously, quivering from head to foot with excitement, but providing little in the way of vivid or varied figure-dancing. For all that a by-stander could tell, they might equally well be walla-bies or wombats or witchetty-grubs. When at last I managed to inquire of a native youth who had some English what it might all be about, I got the unex-pected reply, 'Him'—that is the chorus in its mul-tiple personality—'Him flash-fellow steamer on de ribber'. They were not in the boat, or watching the boat from the bank. They actually were the magnifi-cent creature as it came smoking and splashing up the stream, to the consternation of the black swans. The occasion was purely festive. At the same time, this was at least fine art, if not religion, in the mak-ing. By means of a muscular symbolism they were seeking to express an admiration that might easily ripen into reverence. For the rest, such dancing was bound to react on the whole intellectual and conscious life of the group so as to enlarge it; for the more they learnt to give out in this way, the more they would be competent and eager to take in.

I have said that in the eyes of the natives themselves this was merely a corroboree—a jollification enjoyed for its own sake and apart from any hope of ulterior advantage. I may mention, however, a curious incident that showed how readily a remedial function verging on the miraculous might come to be associated with an entertainment of this type. Some distance away from the dancing-place, under a rough lean-to of boughs, lay an old man, manifestly sick, and in that apathetic state which with the aborigines is usually the prelude to a speedy ending. Instead of worrying him to distraction, as well it might, the loud beat of the dance roused him more and more, so that at last he tottered to his feet and, joining the lively throng, was presently footing it as featly as the rest. Whether in the end it proved a case of kill or cure I never discovered; but I can certainly bear witness to the surprising agility displayed for as long as the dance lasted by an elderly party who a short while before had seemed utterly moribund and done for. Even to me it appeared a miracle that a dose of tribal *joie de vivre* could prove so instantly stimulating. So too, then, it must strike the savage with far greater force in the light of such an experience how dancing in any form is full of *mana.* Inevitably, however, it would be deemed stronger medicine to dance to a deep motif than to dance to a shallow one. A steamer on the Murray is after all no more than the latest sensation. On the other hand, matters of life and death—such as may, broadly speaking, be said to constitute the theme with which religion is perpetually concerned—can be dramatized in exactly the same way, and all the more effectively because emotions more fundamental and vehement than wonder, namely hope and fear, enrich the expression with a note of solemn importance. Thus the sacred dance of Australia stands to the corroboree very much as tragedy does to comedy as regards the dominant feeling-tone. The player plays as if he were in earnest. Though he moves on the plane of mere representation, he must remain in close enough touch with the realities of life to render their essential value and truth; for these realities are as they feel. Thus the sacred dance is bound to bear the character of a mystery; for it has a double meaning like a riddle. It takes a man out of real life, and yet it points back to real life as if it would reveal its secret.

Now, while doubtless it would be possible to classify the sacred ceremonies of the Australians in more than one way, it will be sufficient for our present purpose to divide them into two main types. The difference between these well-marked varieties might be shortly put by saying that in the one case the performers are simply seeking *mana,* and in the other case are seeking it in order to make it work; or even more shortly by saying that in the first case they are trying to be something miraculous, and in the second case to do it. Thus we may term them severally rites of participation and rites of projection. I have myself no hesitation in assigning a ritual character to both kinds of traditional observance alike, in view of the fact that the natives themselves would appear to impute to each very much the same degree of sanctity and virtue. From our point of view, however, the rite of participation is, on the face of it, more like a miracle-play than a religious service, and so might seem intermediate between fine art and religion in form; though the analogy breaks down if we go on to study the intention. Thanks to the searching methods of Spencer and Gillen which have illuminated so many of the obscurities of the aboriginal psychology, we know that the Arunta people of the Central deserts envisage themselves, their customs, the animals and plants on which they live, nay, every water-hole and rock in their bare but hallowed surroundings, against the mellow background of a golden age, the Alcheringa. In those spacious days everybody and everything were splendid in a stone-age way, and, totemistically speaking, all was divine. In a sense, no doubt, those days are over; the glory has departed. But it really makes very little difference whether the golden age is placed in the past or in the future so long as it is likewise conceived as something to live up to in the present. Indeed, the

opposition between past and future can hardly hold
for those who believe in reincarnation, as the Arunta
do. They themselves incorporate Alcheringa beings
who have somehow fallen from their high estate. As
there is no story either of some fault on their part or
of some other fatality that finally debars them from
retrieving the disaster, one might suppose that according to the strict logic of the situation the present
generation might aspire to re-establish the *ancien
régime* without more ado and in their own persons.
But the Arunta have too little logic and too much
sense to suppose anything of the sort. Their present
abode is no Paradise, nor is it likely to become one.
On the other hand, they set up by means of their
dramatic rites a sort of timeless Alcheringa into
which they can turn aside from the hardships of their
present lot, so as to refresh themselves by communion
with transcendent beings who are at once their forefathers and their ideal selves. For the rest it is to be
noted that of distinctive individuality these supermen
of the Alcheringa have almost none. The chorus
seeks simply to glut its collective soul with the
glamour of ancestry—with the consciousness of kind.
The *mana* in which they participate is tribal. As it
was in the beginning, so let the Arunta people be now
and for evermore, Amen.

Passing on to ceremonies of the other type, we may
term them rites of projection because the *mana,*
instead of being assimilated by the performers for
their own spiritual benefit, is transmitted by their

efforts into external things so as to make these work
for their material advantage. Thus among the
Arunta the totemic groups have lost any connexion
that they may once have had with the kinship system,
and act as cult-societies whose function it is to stimulate the reproductive powers of the various animals
and plants that provide man with his food, by showing what is expected of them in explanatory pantomime. The Arunta appear to accept the fact that
nature can be influenced in this way without attempting to account for it. For them it is enough to know
that they can dance themselves into the necessary state
of conviction. The modern theorist, however, is more
inquisitive. Indeed, so much has lately been written
about the symbolism of wish-fulfilment that one may
assume here that the psychology of the matter is
plain, at any rate up to a certain point. One knows
that repressed desire finds an outlet in a simulated
satisfaction, and that the consequent relief of tension
brings about a temporary comfort. But for any wishing of a hopeless or almost hopeless kind such a
remedy but intensifies the disease. The starving man
cannot help dreaming of unlimited food, but to do so
increases his agony in the long run. If there is really
no dinner in the house, to ring the dinner-bell merely
adds insult to injury. On the other hand, in like manner and to a corresponding extent a hopeful kind of
wish may have its hopefulness enhanced by picturing
it as if accomplished. Now it is to be noticed that the
Arunta hold their ceremonies for the multiplication

of the totems, not in the hungry time of the year, but on the contrary when food is plentiful enough for them to gather and be glad together. They dance their food-dances on a full stomach as if to exclaim, 'May this happy state of things continue'. If either prayer or thanksgiving had been known to them in the forms with which we are familiar, one might have looked for as much of the second as of the first in this harvest-festival of the age before agriculture. After all it is a cheerful symbolism that depicts all nature as blowing and growing. No beggar's whine is to be heard in this early religion which prefers to contemplate the bright side of things and to fix it there by the very steadfastness of its gaze. It is quite in accordance with this attitude of unwavering optimism that their rare verbal formulae should exclude the present optative in favour of the perfect indicative. 'We have eaten much food', they say, making solemn pretence meanwhile to eat and be filled. They project their assurance into a kindly, or not too unkindly, universe, and it seems to respond to their hopes in an assured way. They cheer on each other in the dark valley, and a cheerful echo comes back as if a voice from the heights.

In conclusion, a word must be said on a rather trite subject. Many leading anthropologists, including the author of *The Golden Bough,* would wholly or in the main refuse the title of religion to these almost inarticulate ceremonies of very humble folk. I am afraid, however, that I cannot follow them. Nay, I would not leave out a whole continent from a survey of the religions of mankind in order to humour the most distinguished of my friends. Now clearly if these observances are not to be regarded as religious, like a wedding in church, so neither can they be classed as civil, like its drab equivalent at a registry office. They are mysteries, and are therefore at least generically akin to religion. Moreover, they are held in the highest public esteem as of infinite worth whether in themselves or for their effects. To label them, then, with the opprobrious name of magic as if they were on a par with the mummeries that enable certain knaves to batten on the nerves of fools is quite unscientific; for it mixes up two things which the student of human culture must keep rigidly apart, namely, a normal development of the social life and one of its morbid by-products. Hence for me they belong to religion, but of course to rudimentary religion—to an early phase of the same world-wide institution that we know by that name among ourselves. I am bound to postulate the strictest continuity between these stages of what I have here undertaken to interpret as a natural growth. It is quite arbitrary to make religion take shape suddenly out of nothing at the point when Alcheringa beings, totems and so on are supplanted by gods. As well might one say that religion begins when white paint gives way to white ties. Surely a humanizing science must assume that, if men have souls now, they likewise had them in the Stone Age, with needs that at bottom were not so very different.

Of all such needs then, I take hope to be the chief; while I take the stimulation of hope to be the chief function of religion in all its phases. Whether it be chorus or congregation that lifts up its heart in the presence of the sacred, the effect is the same—they go forth to live more dynamically. Having said this much only about religion, then, we have already said a great deal. It remains, however, to examine in subsequent lectures a number of emotional conditions which meet in religious experience, and with various results, some good, some bad, qualify the primal impulse to hope for the sheer joy and intrinsic helpfulness of hoping. Though religion is an exultation, it must likewise be a discipline. It is good that we should hope beyond measure, and yet it is good that there should be a certain measure in such hoping. So far we have been simply considering how religion applies a spur to the life-force. In the sequel we shall have to inquire how far this process, to be thoroughly successful, must also involve the use of a rein.

III

FEAR

*Fear is secondary to hope, if equally fundamental in re-
ligion; its true function being to induce a needful caution,
though in its craven form it is an enemy to strenuous living. Black magic illustrates this bad side; whereas its
good side appears in those disciplinary terrorisms which
religion employs in connexion with punishment, whether
hereafter or on this earth, or again, with the educational
system both at puberty and in later life. Thus fear, giving rise, as it does, to quasi-positive attitudes such as
purity and humility, exerts a chastening force directly
helpful to the good life.*

In the last lecture we saw how hope marks the positive, or forward, pole of the directional energy manifested in our conscious life, and how therefore its
function in religion, which in its emotional aspect is
simply intensified life-feeling, is correspondingly
universal and supreme. There also exists, however, both in conscious experience as a whole, and
in the special form that it assumes under the
stimulating influence of religion, a negative pole,
which is marked by fear. Thus the function of fear
is in its way no less universal or supreme than that of
hope; though, even so, hope is of superior impor-

tance, since ultimately we fear because we hope, and not *vice versa*. This priority in respect to value comes out even more clearly as we ascend the scale that leads from instinct up to reason. The brute, having but the dimmest appreciation of ends, moves on mainly because nature steadily applies the lash of fear to its hind-quarters. The man, on the other hand, being more intelligent, gazes on the whole to his front in pursuit of a good which, however fleeting and elusive in reality, at least displays a substantive appearance. By comparison, then, the evil at his back seems shadowy, since at most he but glances at it over his shoulder. From nothingness to somethingness—such is the meaning of the life-process to a man in proportion as he lives purposively. Only a pessimist could afford to dwell on the thought of the reverse step from somethingness to nothingness; and the pessimist is not among those who shall inherit the earth.

Fears, however, are not all of one type, though undoubtedly they are of one parentage, the father and mother of all fears being, biologically speaking, the fear of death. Nevertheless, the specific difference is great between the two main kinds of fear— the kind that is craven and the kind that is simply cautious. The one forces a man to run away blindly from the danger, the other induces him to try to baffle it by putting forth his cunning. Thus, whereas craven fear stands for bare negation, cautious fear is quasi-positive in its bearing on human activity. The

former paralyses, the latter instructs. Now there
may be good biological excuse for a paralytic attitude on the part of a low organism deficient in
mobility or in the power of counter-attack. The only
chance in such a case is to avoid detection by lying
low. To the animal capable of fighting for its life,
however, not to do so is atavistic, a disloyalty to the
breed—unless indeed the race as a whole is engaged
on the perilous task of organic retrogression. Now
man, with his excellent brain and his skilful hands
supplemented by all sorts of handy tools, is certainly
not anxious to abdicate his present dominance. He
will not take to the downward path, if he can help it.
Indeed, very few, if any, of our descendants would
succeed in getting back to the trees. Hence in the
eyes of the anthropologist who tries to look at human
life in its full perspective, and can make but scant
allowance for exceptional circumstances and temporary conditions, passivity is a policy of the feeble-
minded—a stage on the road to extinction. There are
in odd corners of the world little fading groups of
mild savages who, at any rate as viewed through the
telescope of a philosopher such as Herbert Spencer,
appear quite blameless, although in a strictly negative way. They do nothing wrong, and very little
else; and, in the meantime, they are disappearing
rapidly. Herbert Spencer indeed is wont to contrast
them, by no means to their disadvantage, with those
stirring societies, whether militaristic or industrial,
which will soon have hustled these amiable if anae-

mic quietists from off the face of the earth. Now as
a man he might deplore their fate, but as the philosopher who was the first to inscribe the word 'Evolution' on his banner he was bound to recognize that
such a fate was inevitable. If they had been more
active, not to say aggressive, in their habits, they
would indubitably have improved their chance of
survival. It might perhaps be fanciful to credit these
laggard folk in general with a fear of life; but their
sad example can be cited here as at any rate illustra-
tive of the fact that, for the members of our stock, to
be merely content to keep out of harm's way is of no
use, since the harm will surely search out their hid-
ing-place in the end. To judge by its known history,
our species owes its prosperity and very existence far
more to its positive than to its negative virtues; and,
of all the positive virtues, courage is by right of its
achievements champion.

Courage, however, it must not be forgotten, can be
of the physical, the moral, or the intellectual variety;
and it is rare that three such signal perfections should
meet in the same man. Our modern world worships
physical courage, and offers homage of a more distant
kind to moral courage; but on the whole it may be
said to pay little heed to intellectual courage, which
in the form of a forward-reaching, positive readiness
to grapple with the unknown is perhaps chiefly
responsible for man's conquest over the rest of nature.
To tackle fire, to go to sea on a log, to ride the wild
horse, to fly the Atlantic—these are feats of imagina-

tion even more than they are feats of nerve or of
patience. The true hero is something of a seer. He is
brave to recklessness because he pursues a vision. He
puts his trust in an idea which suggests, though by
the nature of the case it cannot express, a something
good to be gained by closing with the unknown. The
hero is just as much of a positivist as the man who
says that seeing is believing; only he converts the
proposition and holds that believing is seeing ahead.

To apply these considerations to the subject of
primitive religion, let us go back to our original assumption that all religion is concerned with living
in its fundamental character of a life-and-death
struggle. There can be no arguing about the direction; it is given by these cardinal points, life forward,
death behind. So too hope and fear, among our emotional promptings, indicate these two main terminals,
the positive and the negative, of the force—the potential—that moves and has its being in us. Which-
ever way we look from our standpoint of the unstable
present, the far end is enveloped with the darkness
of the unknown. But the horror of the great darkness, for the normal human being, has reference only
to the rearward side—the side of death. He shudders
at the prospect of such blank nothingness; whereas,
though the something that lurks in the other unknown may be anything, he welcomes it as at least
holding out to him the promise of more being.
Rather than die, he will take life gratefully as it
comes. Moreover, so far as we are entitled to speak

of a race-consciousness, we have good reason to attribute to it precisely the same sanguine disposition towards the future. No man, no body of men, really fears to live; but they may easily fail to hope and strive enough. All have a certain liking of the road with its one-way traffic; but many are nervous or slumber at the steering-wheel, and these crash.

Now, whereas I am prepared to submit that fear of the craven type cannot enter into religion at all by reason of its essential hopefulness of outlook, I would like to illustrate the effects of such a fear from religion's disreputable counterpart, namely black magic or sorcery. The sorcerer, though with a different end in view, gets to work on much the same raw material as does the priest. Both of them deal with human nature and, as far as the emotions go, with complexes of these that show the strongest family likeness. Both stir the soul by playing on the life-and-death *motif;* but, whereas the priest seeks to intensify the life-feeling, the sorcerer's object is to intensify the death-feeling. Which of the two operates with the more conspicuous success in savage society it is hard to say; for some brands of killing magic would seem to be remarkably sure in their results. Thus Dr. Roth was so impressed by what he saw in Queensland of the complete inhibition of the will to live induced in his native patients by the thought of being under a spell that he coined the word *thanatomania* in order to do justice to this suicidal fatalism—this unnatural craze for giving up the ghost.

Now of course the most talented exponent of the art of bedevilling his neighbours cannot manufacture this morbid discouragement out of nothing at all. There must be on the part of the victim a certain faint-heartedness, a disposition to believe the worst, such as might be due to individual weakness of character, but is more often a result of the state of the social atmosphere at the moment. Primitive communities easily succumb to a conviction that they are witch-ridden; and indeed it was no other phobia than this which caused christian Europe and America in comparatively recent times to exhibit all the symptoms of temporary insanity. Whereas, however, our witch-burners, with their religion of charity, and with such natural science as they already possessed, had every reason to be ashamed of their hysterical excesses, a horde of savages with nothing but their custom, and a few miles of country, between them and the utterly unknown, might well be more subject to panic than they actually are. Moreover, under very primitive conditions, the crowd can find a way out of the trouble far more easily than the individual. Acting in their collective capacity they can practise rites, they can observe taboos, or at the worst they can clear the air—in other words, rouse their spirits—by means of a public witch-hunt. But the individual who has private reasons for feeling upset—for instance, because an unfriendly person has glared at him, or because he has been visited with a twinge of the rheumatics—can fall back on no such well-established and easily tapped resources. Primitive religion, being almost wholly communal, does not enable the individual to dance himself back into fortitude by means of a *pas seul*. He has, of course, his amulets, his personal taboos, and so on, to furnish him with a *mana* of his very own; but, in the case of the average man at any rate, his luck, like his usefulness, amounts to very little apart from the support and co-operation of his fellows. An exceptional man, on the other hand, is likely to be a bit of a sorcerer himself; or at any rate will be ready, if he thinks himself threatened, to start a vigorous counter-offensive. Thus the self-confident man meets the machinations of hatred with scorn; but curses, undoubtedly, can kill cowards.

Before leaving the subject of craven fear, we should notice how, just as it is courage of the intellectual variety that is largely responsible for human progress, so it is the corresponding kind of fear, an imaginative fear, or fear of the uncanny, which can thus conjure up for the ignorant savage the grim form of the messenger of death. However physically tough, he is mentally tender. The shrewdest blow on his thick pate will hardly make him wince; whereas he is delicately sensitive to the slightest hint of mystery. Let me be pardoned if I recall a trifling incident from my own experience which, though of a kind familiar to every field-worker, will serve to illustrate my point well enough. We were visiting a mixed lot of Australian natives in a reservation. They had evidently made acquaintance with hymn-books and harmoniums; and, altogether, were sophisticated and tame to a fault. There seemed no possible harm, therefore, in persuading one of them, an old man, to sing some corroboree songs which he remembered into the mouth of a phonograph; and presently we treated him to the record of his own voice, expecting at the best delighted admiration, or at the worst unfavourable comment on the quality of our instrument. It turned out, however, that, for the reservation in question, phonographs still were parcels of the dread unknown. When his own voice came back to him out of the machine, the old man changed colour as if his heart had stopped beating. We had the greatest trouble to reassure him. Luckily the little crowd of natives, women as well as men, was not homogeneous enough to afford sympathetic support to his reaction; and we were thankful to some tittering native girls who decidedly helped to break the spell. At last, a rather laboured explanation that a phonograph was a white man's message-stick on which one marked down anything that one wanted to repeat seemed to go home to the intelligence of the victim of science; and I trust that he found his personality not seriously diminished by the tax which he had levied upon it. Yet what a frail thing is a human soul— *animula vagula blandula*—thus to flicker like an uncertain flame at the slightest breath of a suggestion of evil, when the root of the evil is ignorance, a weakness of the inner man! It may even be that the average human being has always been somewhat chicken-hearted in regard to what no plain fellow can be expected to understand. Certainly our anthropological text-books provide us with a vast miscellany of things which some savage at some time has listed under the category of the mysterious, and hence the more or less tabooed. But, on the principle that one hero can make a regiment brave, there have always been adventurous spirits, more far-gazing than the rest, if not necessarily more far-seeing, in respect to their powers of imagination, who steeling their bosoms against doubt, advanced to explore the mystery and, if possible, to find treasure in the heart of it. One must, therefore, not be too hard on that ambiguous character, the reputed sorcerer, even while agreeing that his unsavoury reputation with his comrades is sometimes well deserved. How many a primitive inventor must likewise have had reason to regret his odd proceedings! To find solace for its sense of inferiority in doing a great man to death is a time-honoured expedient with the common herd; and, so long as the difference between a malefactor and a martyr depends on the opinion of a jury of plain men, mistakes will occur such as are only perceptible, if at all, to the historian of the future. At best, then, the crowd is competent to judge in a rough-and-ready way whether the conduct of one who breaks away from custom is, or is not, to its own immediate advantage. Thus the very same dabbler in the occult who may be suspected of black magic will at some other time have to be called in as an exorcist in order to counteract the spells imputed to a rival practitioner; while the measure of his unstable popularity will doubtless be in direct ratio with the number of his cures. Or, again, a man of light and leading, whom it would not do to offend lest he be tempted to employ his art in a private way, may lawfully and with the favour of all let loose his power of blasting and blighting on the public enemy, whether a tribesman who has violated the law, or the unspeakable foreigner who lives across the border. Thus it is easier in theory than in its practical application to draw a distinct line between the spheres of magic and religion, if we try to adjust our standard of scientific judgement to the valuation of the people concerned. They recognize, and rightly, a hateful kind of terrorism based on a criminal exploitation of the strange and dire; and, while for the most part they cannot stand up to it individually at all, but abjectly meet their doom half-way, in their corporate capacity they contrive a counterblast by executing some one who may, possibly, be the guilty party. Side by side, however, with such an illegal form of terrorism, they recognize another kind, which, equally ready as it is to enlist the fear of the unknown in its service, is nevertheless the reputable instrument of law and order. Thus, while the two terrorisms agree closely in method, their motives are as completely divided as is vice from virtue.

At this point we may fitly pass on to consider the

function of fear as it enters into religion so as to assist
it in its character of a discipline. For religion, although it is instinct with hopefulness and the promise
of life, also involves what may truly be termed a
terrorism, since it threatens the backslider, the man
who will not attend to its call to live intensely, with
the merciless alternative, an intensified death, dam-
nation, a death without peace. But its threat is not
absolute like that of the sorcerer, who would bring
about a craven fear, the utter negation of hope. On
the contrary, it is a conditional threat, inducing a
fear that is intended to be but precautionary. There
must always be some hope left for the repentant, if
religion is to fulfil its mission. Otherwise in the
extravagance of its comminations it belies its true
nature, and as the ally of despair must be reckoned
along with sorcery as a morbid development of mind
and society. On the other hand, it is a normal requirement of any social institution, or any system of
education, that it should use fear as a menace; for
human beings will neither strive to co-operate nor to
learn unless forcible means are taken to keep them up
to the mark. In all such cases there must be a tradition, a set of working rules such as past experience
recommends; and the infringement of these rules
must be prevented by means of suitable penalties.
In short, there must be a law; and a law is no law
without a sanction.

In the rest of this lecture, then, let us touch on
these three topics in turn, the idea of a hell, the main-

tenance of society, and the system of moral education, in order to test the quality of the associated fear in each case. By so doing we ought to be able to make out something like an ascending scale of values, as the fear is perceived to display less of the deadliness of the raw article, which is simply a poison, and more of the invigorating and even palatable effects which, when used judiciously as a tonic, it can lend to a draught duly sweetened with hope. For religion needs to institute in its own interest a branch of investigation corresponding to what is known to medical science as Posology, the study of the quantities in which drugs should be administered in order to secure the best results. An overdose of fear in the life-potion which it is the business of religion to supply can in no way make for spiritual health; while it may even persuade stricken folk that unassisted nature is more tolerable than the doctor.

Now to consider in the first place the idea of hell, it is perhaps easier to find reasons why such a notion should have arisen than to account for the opposite belief in a happy hereafter, a heaven. For death encountered in the flesh is not a beautiful but a ghastly sight; nor, on the plane of a merely animal intelligence, is its foulness anything but a warning to the living to keep away, seeing that human beings have not the entrails of hyenas. It was indeed a triumph of the gregarious instinct, not to rate it higher, when it led the lowly savage to open the first chapter of recorded history by laying out his dead in state.

By a noble lie they hushed up the truth both about the dead man's pitiful condition and about their own no less pitiful desolation, disguising the inhospitable tomb as an abode of peace and comfort. Thus they cheated death of its natural right to be the king of terrors; yet possibly not for long. Whether they saw ghosts more frequently than we do, it is hard to be sure; but, as often as it came to them, this experience cannot have been less daunting than it is for the educated man of to-day, while the chances are that it would throw them far more completely off their mental balance. 'Come back to us if you will in dreams,' cries the Australian native to his dead kinsman at the final leave-taking, 'but not as a ghost.' If then, one's nearest and dearest were thus unwelcome in a spectral form, what of the far more repellent shapes of murderous foes, of mischievous and malignant wizards, or of hunters untimely slain by wild beasts, and young mothers cut off in childbirth —unhappy wights with a perpetual grievance against their more fortunate brethren. The former might be trusted to leave their own folk alone; unless indeed they received special invitations to attend some feast of All Souls, or else had some definite act of neglect or disrespect on the part of their relatives of which to make complaint. But the latter could be no better than fiends, vampires, ghouls, the miscreants and outcasts of the apparitional world. Hence, as Tylor has so well shown, primitive eschatologies, starting from a view of the hereafter as simply the continuation of this life, pass on readily to a theory of idealized continuation, on the dualistic principle that one's friends are like to fare better than before, and one's enemies worse. From this to an embryonic theory of retribution is but a step; for since one's friends are naturally good and one's enemies bad, unequal distribution of their future happiness seems to be eminently just. Finally, some sort of last judgement at which each soul must reap reward or punishment according to its personal and particular deserts is clearly conceived—so clearly, in fact, that an obliging savage will sometimes draw a map to show exactly where along the trail of the dead the stern judge stands and the path divides. It is to be noted, too, that such beliefs often occur among peoples of lowly culture amongst whom there is small opportunity for individuality to develop in a general way. Doubtless the explanation is that, as men die one by one, so they are held to be examined one by one. For the rest it need hardly be said that the oddest qualifications are apt to prevail with a savage Rhadamanthus. Thus, a way from the Assam Hills to heaven is open to any gallant who has seven successful love-affairs to his credit. Often, too, the moral value of the claim is not apparent, as when it rests on a handsome funeral, or a well-embroidered suit of tattoo. In such cases, no doubt, the assumption is that consideration will be shown towards persons of quality. Meanwhile, whatever be the way in which some are saved, others are on such a view to all eternity damned. One cannot but detect more kindliness, therefore, in the alternative doctrine of a reincarnation which allows the failures to try again, profiting by an experience of the wages of sin which has perhaps been quickened in some intermediate purgatory. Indeed, even when an implacable hell finds a place in a primitive mythology, no organized attempt is made to bring its horrors home to the imagination, and thereby to tyrannize over the soul, as among advanced peoples who, professedly, have ceased to hate their enemies or at least to torture them. At all events, the refined paganism of a Plato could seriously propose to scrap Styx, Cocytus, Tartarus, and all such bugaboos of the infernalist, on the express ground that to render the hero-temper susceptible to so base a kind of fear is not to strengthen and educate it, but to undermine and destroy its strength.

Turning to the office of religious fear as a supporter of the social authority, this is bound to appear salutary or sinister according as it is associated either with a reasonable form of discipline or with a crushing despotism. Now for the historian of civilization there must be great difficulty at times in deciding whether at a given stage in the development of a large and powerful society the amount of brute force exerted by those in control was justified or not; the test of course being whether the people in question thereafter emerged into freedom, or sank into servility and decay. Happily the anthropologist who restricts himself to the study of savagery or at most of barbarism has small experience of the type of society of which the appropriate blazon would be a bloody sword crossed with a red-hot poker. Perhaps tropical Africa is the only part of his beat where such a phenomenon may be encountered; and even so a close examination usually tends to mitigate the facts reported from a region where undoubtedly life is cheap and punishments are cruel. On the other hand, what is usually described as the lower savagery is in the main remarkably free from the use of the oppressor's rod; nor can it truly be urged by way of counterclaim that these ungoverned folk are ungovernable in their ways. Though custom is their only king, they are as loyal to it as if it had the executioner at its elbow. Moreover, in its regulative capacity custom is as potent on its negative as on its positive side. 'Thou shalt not' is indeed far more conspicuously and categorically enunciated than 'Thou shalt.' But the threat which forms the sanction of the typical taboo is largely implicit. The bare suggestion of an indefinite evil attending its violation ensures an unquestioning obedience. There are no sceptics, and therefore there is no hell-fire.

Yet, although wellnigh automatic in its action, taboo none the less inevitably consigns the offender to his just doom. Even when human hands are not available to second the operation of the curse, as when kindred blood has been shed, and the relatives can do nothing because they dare not duplicate the sin, there are Furies in reserve that will harry the outcast as he leaves his home for the outer darkness. Or when society finds itself able to intervene, and the abandoned of heaven is purged out of existence by the agency of the powers on earth, the dominant significance remains that of a sacrifice; so that the fear can mingle with a certain pity for the victim as though at the spectacle of a tragedy—the downfall of a human being who has too rashly wrestled with fate. It may not exactly accord with our notions of political education thus to exalt the majesty of the law in a way so little calculated to bring out its utilitarian function. Yet, thanks to his religion, the savage knows that he must or must not, long before he is capable of learning why. No doubt the result is that primitive codes abound with arbitrary prescriptions, moral and purely ritual requirements being jumbled together in wild confusion; while the sanctity of the whole forbids all rational reformation of the parts. Granting all this, however, the balance of advantage would seem to lie with the theory of a sacred and therefore inviolable law, so long as mankind is devoid of letters and must trust for its traditional rules to mere memory, supplemented by religion in the form of a drill-sergeant. An attention hardly less muscular than mental is needed to enable the body politic to be smart and effective on such an insistent war-service as Hobbes truly represented the state of nature to be. Primitive religion issues its orders with the necessary sharpness, and enforces them by means of the sheer impressiveness of its mien. It may be harsh; it may be even inclined to bully. Yet all, to the latest-joined recruit, are proud of it. It is theirs; it is the Regiment. After all, it intends to make men of them, and it surely will.

To proceed, finally, to the subject of education, it is obvious from what has just been said about the severity of the social drill involved in a régime of sacrosanct custom that, if the adult is beaten with rods, the youth is likely to be beaten with scorpions. The child, indeed, is treated with great indulgence, perhaps because he is regarded as not yet ripe for religion. When puberty comes, however, an initiation has normally to be faced during which a series of most unpleasant experiences, both physical and moral, has to be endured by the candidates for manhood with as much fortitude as they can summon to their aid. No doubt a good deal of positive instruction in regard to their future duties accompanies this organized intimidation. The tribal elders, in fact, to use an agricultural metaphor which they might not understand, are but scarifying the soil in order that it may the better receive the good seed of their counsel. So much indeed is this the case that the simple devices employed to overawe the freshman are blandly revealed to him as soon as he has taken his degree. The weird sound, for instance, which at first he, as also his mother, took to be the voice of Hobgoblin coming to eat him, is duly explained at the end of his trial, when a bull-roarer is put into his

hand and he is sent off to scare the women by whirling it round to his heart's content. Yet it must not
be supposed that because a mask is thus removed, a
veil lifted, it is implied that the rest of the tribal
solemnities are so much empty hocus-pocus. On the
contrary, as in the Australian case just noticed, the
whole of a man's life is conceived as a series of initiations into a mystery which deepens as the symbolism
becomes more refined—that is, better adapted to the
needs of a mature intelligence. The stage at which
the material bull-roarer can be used to frighten a boy
is done with; but that does not prevent the same boy,
when he has become an old man, full of religious
wisdom and zeal, from believing that when he goes
about 'singing' the grass in order to make it grow
he is 'full of *churinga*'—full of what the *churinga*
or bull-roarer stands for, namely, an inward and
spiritual grace, *mana*. Such a man can, in the consciously or half-consciously metaphorical language
of the Arunta, possess within himself an *ertnatu-
lunga,* a whole storehouse of sacred things, demate-
rialized yet no less substantially present and sustaining. Despite their short-comings in the way of
abstract phraseology, these stone-age folk have managed to make clear to themselves that what is but a
toy, if taken literally, can suggest, when taken in its
full religious sense, the very inwardness of the tribal
mysteries, that power which, according to their own
testimony, makes them feel 'glad' and 'good' and
'strong'. A man of ripe experience, a tribal elder,

who has advanced far enough in his religious development to realize its object so distinctly, may well have put aside fear in its cruder and more childish forms once and for all; even if he still deems it useful as a means of managing children. On the other hand, such a man has in no sense broken with the discipline of taboo, but practices austerities which he freely acknowledges to be necessary if he is to preserve his spiritual health. Already, then, at this low level of a muscular ritualism barely illuminated by a few dim notions, fear has, in the course of a life-long education, not in theology but in the school of religious practice, become sublimated into the fear of defilement, no longer a negative but a quasi-positive feeling. Spiritual purity, like physical cleanliness, is no mere absence of dirt, but something that can be enjoyed for its own sake. Like liberty, another quasi-positive feeling which it closely resembles, it imparts a sense of poise. Being relieved of various contacts and frictions, the inner man has a better chance of finding his feet. Moreover, since as soon as he has found his feet he will assuredly strike out, purity, which is quasi-positive, is half-way to positive power—to the dynamical mood.

It remains to say a word about humility. This essentially religious virtue is also quasi-positive—a conditional clause in a charter conveying a grant. It stands for the fact that all greatness of soul involves an 'if'. In short, humility is a due sense of the difficulties of the spiritual way of life. There must be enough respect for his adversary in the brave man's composition to make him train for the fight. Such conditional, precautionary fear, then, simply braces and does not hamper. But humility, like purity, can be overdone. Many types of mind produced by a religious education show signs of over-training—of overdoing the salutary process of toughening and starving, until a nervous wretch is produced who is permanently incapable of putting forth his inborn maximum effort. Once more, then, we come back to the conclusion that terrorism, the abuse of fear, is always a morbid symptom in religious development, and one that becomes increasingly sinister as religion grows more capable of appealing to a refined intelligence. From its savage days religion has retained a blood-and-thunder style of expression which may still impress the vulgar but can only offend the spiritual susceptibilities of educated men. Our theologians, then, might take a hint from native Australia, and, at any rate when religious initiation has reached a certain stage, should explain away their bull-roarers and hob-goblins as so many rattles and gollywogs, which, though playing their proper part in nursery education, cannot possibly provide the symbolism capable of suggesting to an adult mind the true meaning of the fear of God. Perhaps a study of the natural history of religion may help them in this their task of brave and honest expurgation.

IV

LUST

In seeking to regularize the violence of sexual emotion, religion has been less concerned to encourage than to restrain it. The repressions involved in the incest-taboo may go back to a matri-central form of the family, when the mother's blood, being regarded as the sole source of generation, provoked an awe that enabled her to enforce chaste relations within the home circle. In contrast marriage, being at first little more than a tolerated license, developes rites that are partly piacular, though partly making for communion between alien groups. As male ascendancy grows, the fertility cult gives way to forms of religion that reflect masculine authority.

FROM a biological point of view, the deepest mystery of life consists in its power of self-propagation in a related series of individual forms. Correspondingly we find that the most intense hopes and fears of humanity are concerned with the subject of generation, which in the conception of living as a life-and-death affair stands for the 'and'—the pivotal point of connexion on which our feelings sway backwards and forwards between the joy of being continued and the sorrow of being left behind and cut off. Religion, then, is bound in its symbolic way to emphasize this antinomy, as also to do its best to resolve it, by lifting up the idea of birth from the physical to the spiritual plane. In so doing, however, it finds it hard to extend the same process of sublimation to the attendant notion of sex, the physical associations of which are too strong to submit readily to analogical reinterpretation. Thus a connotation of uncleanness comes to attach to the biological source of our being, and Nature and God appear to be at strife over a business which at any rate has the full approbation of our animal instincts. It follows that, in an historical survey such as we are attempting now, it is lust as something to be overcome, rather than sexual love as something to be encouraged, that will chiefly be in evidence, when the emotional attitude of religion towards the procreative act comes under review. For the anthropologist, indeed, no question arises as to whether religion is morally right or wrong in lending its support to a certain sexlessness as a condition of the serious life. His duty is simply to elicit from the facts whether it has this tendency or not; and the facts are to some extent contradictory, seeing that, if religion favours celibacy, it likewise consecrates marriage. On the whole, however, it looks as if human experience in its religious form had found it more profitable, in the sense of more conducive to the actual maintenance of life, to ration rather than to pamper the most greedy of the appetites. Certain it is at all events that here lies the crux of the problem how to humanize our animal nature—how to incarnate the spiritual by the disincarnation of the bestial.

Now a casual observer of savage life is apt to imagine it a welter of amatory confusion. Nay, responsible theorists have vied with each other in depicting a primal condition of society when marriage simply was not, and the habits of the barnyard or the rabbit-warren predominated instead. Whether termed crudely promiscuity, or cryptically hetairism, or pedantically agamy, or euphemistically communal marriage, or delicately primitive indifference, the state of affairs thus variously indicated was such as must have caused the student of early man to blush, had any power of television enabled him to look upon it. Fortunately, he has been spared the unseemly sight, and in the meantime is too busy to listen to disreputable stories about forerunners whose historical status is about on a par with that of the fairies. On the other hand, the real savage as we observe him is so far from being a votary of free love that he is rather the victim of an all-too-legal matrimony. Relentless taboos claim his life in forfeit if, however involuntarily, he violates the letter of their prescriptions. The dread name of incest attaches to the slightest breach of the regulations that forbid unions between kinsfolk, even though these are reckoned so by a convention having but a remote reference to the actual ties of blood. So universal and so profound is the horror caused by such a type of sin that the whole community deems itself polluted until an expiatory sacrifice is made by expunging the sinner. Such facts are well known to every anthropologist, though his knowledge abruptly ceases at the point at which the explanation of them begins. One school of thought is inclined to postulate a beneficent instinct against in-breeding; although this has, confessedly, been somewhat diverted from its biological aim by interference on the part of the primitive legislator. The other school, led by Freud, insists that the closest kind of in-breeding is permitted, nay recommended strongly, by nature, but that man in his wisdom or unwisdom has bound himself fast in the chains of an artificial system; the very terrorism associated with its enactments proving that their tenor is wholly against the grain. Far be it from me to spoil a good fight by proposing to arbitrate between opponents so well matched. I would merely note in passing that, in asserting that the trend of instinct is away from close interbreeding, or towards it, each party has passed beyond social anthropology into the more spacious region of biological genetics; while neither of them, so far as I know, had been at the pains to show by detailed reference to human history whether the cross-bred or the in-bred stocks—and in a relative sense such can with sufficient clearness be distinguished—have on the whole and in the long run had the better of it in the struggle for existence. While, however, the decision on these ultimate and almost transcendental questions is pending, we may at least take note of the fact that, whereas science still disputes, primitive religion has made up its mind. It might almost be said to declare, by the vigour that it puts into the enforcement of decidedly inconsistent principles, that any law prohibing incest is better than none at all.

Now, in the voluminous literature that exists on this subject, it is curious that all the stress should be laid on marriage as the constitutive ground of the taboo against incest—the substantive good which this mass of negative injunctions is implicitly designed to further. Indeed, it is usual to describe them comprehensively as the laws of exogamy, as if the positive precept involved was, 'Marry out.' But this is to view the matter from the wrong end. The true commandment is, 'Be chaste within the home circle.' In a sense the incest-taboo takes no interest in marriage whatsoever. So long as correct relations are observed within the kinship group, what goes on outside in the way of licit or illicit love is of no concern to the law. Thus when Lord Avebury in his picturesque way speaks of the Australian being entitled to 'a thousand miles of wives', he merely means, or at any rate ought to mean, that, even when he is on a journey and in the enjoyment of a certain kind of traditional hospitality, the native must rigorously avoid even a temporary liaison with a member of the group corresponding to his totem or matrimonial class. The same requirement holds good of those so-called supplementary unions characteristic of the Lake Eyre tribes, in which some authorities—though I do not agree with them—would have us recognize a survival of group-marriage. I could almost wish, however, that this theory were sound, so well would it in that case serve to illustrate my point. For there is nothing in the law of exogamy as it exists among these tribes or among any others to prohibit utter promiscuity outside what American writers are fond of describing as the incest-group. A nicer phrase, however, which at any rate will serve my present purpose, is the home circle. For nomad peoples, indeed, no home in a local sense can very well be said to exist; but there is always a social group, a more or less coherent body of messmates of both sexes, in whose midst the individual feels at home as nowhere else. Paradoxical as it may sound to us, the primitive view of intimacy is that it excludes the possibility of sexual commerce. We need hardly go out of our way, as for instance Durkheim has done, to saddle some obscure superstition about blood with the whole responsibility for a restraint so obviously bound up with the discipline of a stable and effective symbiosis. The choice lay between an ever-rampant jealousy and concord, and concord proved the more solid attraction. The exclusiveness of sexual appetite being incompatible with any constancy of sympathetic give-and-take, one of the two had to go under, and, fortunately for the future of humanity, the feeling of kin prevailed, to become the nucleus round which a whole phase of the organization of society was presently to develop.

Now it is hard for us, who for better or worse seem

committed to the family, the nuclear combination of papa, mamma, and baby, to conceive the ideal home in terms of a domestic continence tempered by extraneous, casual, and almost furtive amours. Yet under mother-right in its extremer form, when the woman—one hesitates to say the wife—cleaves to her kin, while the male-element, singular or plural, must play the barely tolerated visitor, the romance of life, if it exists anywhere at all, is certainly not to be found in conjugal affection. But, because she is hardly a wife, the woman is none the less a mother. Though the word matriarchy is a bad one—only one degree less bad, in fact, than Bachofen's beloved gynaecocracy—it conveys a modicum of truth; even if it has to be qualified by the use of a third phrase no less portentous, the avunculate—meaning the united strength of mother's big brothers. In its executive capacity, perhaps, the kin is primarily a brotherhood. In another aspect, however, it is a motherhood, and there can be little doubt that this was the view of it taken on the whole by the earliest religion. We touch here, no doubt, on very speculative matters. Strabo's naïve statement that all men allow woman to have been the foundress of religion is neither here nor there; for Strabo and his friends were no better informed on the question at issue than ourselves. At the same time it is likely enough that woman always had her say, and even the chief say, in regard to sexual matters. One has heard a great deal lately about the patriarch of the Cyclopean horde who in his own interest enforces a one-sided and therefore unstable continence upon his younger group-fellows. Granting that male jealousy and rivalry are basic facts which must be duly taken into account, one may still wonder why so little is made of the complementary evidence relating to the part played by the female in sexual selection. That this is not a wholly passive rôle is known to every biologist, even if his comparative studies do not carry him so far as anthropology. Meanwhile, to regard the human female, even in a love-affair of the so-called 'cave-man' type, as incapable of effective rejection, despite her physical inferiority, would be to put her below the level of her counterpart in many another animal species. Assuredly she could baffle the most importunate of her suitors by the simple threat of withdrawing the light of her countenance. Indeed one may even hazard the guess that the initiative in the skirmishes preceding the real affair lay with the lady all the time, even if nature taught her the art of masking her batteries. Instinct, in other words, bade her surround herself with mystery, and she may well have appeared half-goddess and half-devil from the earliest times to the mere man. Even regarded simply as the object of his sexual desire, she could but seem a blessing and a plague in one.

But woman has a second string to her bow. If she is mysterious as a mistress, she is doubly so as a mother. It may seem incredible that savages at the mental level of the Australian or New Guinea tribes should fail to connect conjugation and parturition as physiological cause and effect; but the evidence, after much adverse criticism, has been found to stand. So long, then, as human society remained unable to put two and two together on this subject, every birth in their eyes must have seemed a parthenogenesis or, at all events, a gynaecogenesis. From first to last the woman had all the responsibility and all the credit for the creation of new human life. Thus not merely in a titular sense but literally, the mother stood for the fountain-head of the matrilineal group. The men in their superior way might elaborate a mythology concerning the esoteric reasons why babies are born; but she was bound to get the benefit of it, seeing that it was all about her and about her only. Economically considered no doubt the male counted for a good deal; but viewed cosmically he was but as the rainbow in the waterfall—an epiphenomenon in the absence of which the movement of life could proceed just as merrily as ever.

Further, the division of labour between the sexes is strictly observed in primitive life; and religion was not slow to sanction an arrangement which perceptibly worked. One hears, it is true, mostly about the male side of the inter-sexual taboo—how a woman who interferes with masculine concerns puts a blight on them; so that on his own confession the strong man becomes as feeble and incalculable as she manifestly is herself. When our lady anthropologists have really got into touch with their savage sisters, one hopes to obtain an equally spirited description of the reverse side of the shield. On obstetrical occasions, for instance, the clumsy assistance of the male is rarely in request, unless indeed he has attained to a doctorate which confers a more or less sexless status on the man or woman that holds it. Not to labour the point further, there are functions in which one sex participates to the almost complete exclusion of the other; and correspondingly the mysteries of religion have a dual character, the excluded sex in each case proportioning its awe to its ignorance of the other's secrets. Here, then, was the female portion of the group—the women's camp, so to speak—in the strong position of being the sole accredited agency in charge of the all-important matter of genetics, with the male portion ready to believe that it was nothing less than a meta-genetics. One may be excused for dealing picturesquely with hypothetical beginnings that strict science cannot validate, so that the only alternative is to portray them in a kind of Platonic myth. It is sober truth enough, however, that the mother-goddess has a long history—so long, indeed, that one is inclined to rate her not only as the mother of men, but as the mother of the gods as well. I cannot refrain from mentioning how in the Island of Guernsey there stands, where I have often seen it, an even now most venerable statue-menhir, showing the full breasts of a nursing mother. It was disinterred some half-century ago from beneath the chancel of an ancient church; and many an invocation to the Virgin Mother has been sung over the resting-place where doubtful converts must have hidden it. This idol, with many like specimens of Neolithic age, is in its turn strongly reminiscent of those far more ancient female figurines in ivory or stone which in Late Palaeolithic times must almost certainly have been connected with some kind of fertility cult. Motherhood, then, was certainly a mystery in the days of old; even if it can never be certain that it first became so when, in place of the family, the unit of society was the kin, and the kin was in itself motherhood pure and simple.

To go back, then, to the question how exogamy, or rather the incest-taboo, arose, is it not possible that it was no Cyclopean sire of the type imagined by Atkinson and Freud, but some even more revered kin-mother who is to be hailed as the first to bring primal lust under the reign of law? *Cherchez la femme.* If the women chose, they could always tear to pieces the nascent society, the almost unorganized mother-kin, by stirring up one jealous suitor against another. When they chose to do so no longer, was it at the instance of the males, so peaceful a lot by nature, or was it because they themselves wanted peace in the home—not to speak of decency? As I conceive the Eldest of the Mothers, she was something of a witch, and, however inarticulate, carried curses in her eye. While she had the girls under her hand, she had the boys under this eye of hers, so that they would be well advised to slink off to their amourettes beyond the range of her dire disapprobation.

But, however it came about, somehow within that narrow circle of intenser social life lust once for all was stayed. It had been transformed into incest, an accursed thing. Henceforth lust within the kin was as bad as murder or worse. Both were utterly abominable; for both were offences against the blood, the sacred blood, the blood of the mothers, the blood from which men are born.

In the same context a singular phenomenon must be noticed. In very low societies we occasionally hear of periods of licence when the laws of exogamy are deliberately broken. Many indeed of the so-called sexual orgies of which primitive peoples are accused will on careful inspection turn out to be hardly worse than ebullitions of the carnival spirit; but in certain cases it would seem that custom tolerates, nay, enforces in the name of religion, direct defiance of the curse of the blood. Whereas, then, the saturnalia of the more ordinary type can be explained readily enough in terms of repressed desire and its release, these radical abnormalities of savage life are at first sight harder to understand. It would seem that when they occur in Australia they are tried as a last resource in times of great trouble. It is as if the people hoped to complete the cycle and bring things round to being right again by making them still more wrong. The native theory, however, so far as one exists, is quite obscure, and at most one can make out a vague belief to the effect that a temporary reversion to the ways of the golden age will renew their prosperity. Now of course it would be quite impossible to treat this as a case of genuine folk-memory embodying some age-long tradition of the days before there was any law of incest. There being room, then, only for a psychological as contrasted with a historical interpretation, we must put an additional burden on the theory of repressions, and regard this as an indirect testimony to the strength of the effort required to hold down lust even in the bosom of the uterine family. Equally too may it be taken as a negative proof that religion was the cause of this moral revolution; for only what primitive religion has emphatically affirmed is it liable to contradict with like emphasis in the course of that violent oscillation of emotional tone to which it is subject in its cruder and more hysterical forms. For the method of religion is to stifle lust by generating another kind of lust; and, though carnal lust was effectually routed in this the first battle of a long series, the other kind of passion that won the day was not yet spiritualized enough to advance in a conscious and constant direction.

Passing on to consider the attitude of primitive religion towards marriage, we have to start from the proposition already laid down that, according to the primal law of chastity, there exists a substantive duty to observe continence within the kin-circle; whereas it is beyond its scope to formulate the alternative as a positive scheme of conduct. From such a point of view, then, marriage is at best a kind of chartered

libertinism. It is a method by which two chaste kins
are enabled to enter into an unchaste relation. Let it
be remembered, too, that when such liaisons were at
first tolerated, there was probably no idea of their
physiological consequences. Thus they could hardly
be more than dissipations at which custom winked,
in pursuance of a general policy to allow human
nature an occasional fling, while insisting on the strictest respectability at other times. Even when mother-
right was beginning to give way to father-right, and
that intermediate position had been reached when the
woman lives with the man's kindred, though the child
in name and status still belongs to her own, there was
at best a grudging acknowledgement on the part of
religion that a decent and honourable tie had been
contracted. Thus those tumultuous representations
of a mock capture which form so frequent a feature
of early marriage ceremonies may possibly be *rites
de passage*—dramatic attempts to show that the
woman is exchanging one home for another; but they
bear a suspicious resemblance to a solemnly attested
outrage, a sort of dramatized rape of the Sabines
which implies no concession to female modesty but
rather a concession to the salacity, and even sadism,
of the male. For the primal law of chastity did not
apply to the foreign woman; let her be visited or let
her be carried off, she was still her lover's plaything.
For the rest, since the woman wanted the man less
than he wanted her, and he was in any case the
stronger and more ardent party, he had his way with

her in the end, and she must part all-unwillingly from her own people to bear the lot of the outcast which could be little better than that of a domestic slave. Propitiated with gifts, a sort of blood-money, her kinsmen let her go, such gifts in their earliest form doubtless taking the form of similar offerings, namely the sisters of the strangers. First the animosities of rape and counter-rape; then the formalities of a cold-blooded exchange; and only as a last and most difficult step, the amenities of a friendly alliance—such may well have been the three stages of the evolution of father-right.

What, then, of the consecration of marriage by religion? Has it not always, in sympathy with its primeval tendency, been inclined to avert its face from a lustful proceeding which, however consonant with the promptings of nature, or with the conventions of civil society, nevertheless remains a perpetual scandal in the eyes of the pure; who would be celibate or at most parthenogenetic, if they could, in their relations with the life-process? If one confines one's attention to the most primitive peoples, marriage rites of a sacramental kind are not greatly in evidence; while it not infrequently happens that cohabitation begins with hardly any ceremonial recognition of the fact on the part of the social groups concerned, however much they may have quietly led up to the affair by previous treaty. Even when one goes on to consider more advanced communities, it is to be noted how many of the rites wear a piacular appearance, as if, instead of helping to tie the knot more firmly, they would rather neutralize the shame of a licentious connexion. No doubt the object of ceremonies of this negative type may be partly to get rid of personal shyness on the part of the man and woman about to be initiated into the mysteries of sex, and it is for this reason that the anthropologist is wont to envisage marriage chiefly, after our modern fashion, as a crisis of the individual life, as indeed it truly is. But for primitive folk we may suspect that the social view of an institution ever tends to predominate. Nay, this is so even when it relates to a strictly individual affair such as birth or death, and not one which like marriage is inter-individual, that is to say, contractual. Now when two kins assist at the marriage of a pair of its members there is a great deal to be neutralized in the sheer amount of mutual suspicion and dislike that any meeting of rival groups is bound to entail. Religion, then, which is always ready to act as a civil servant, though without much display of enthusiasm for its task, must see to it that a truce is patched up; that the consentient parties do not turn the bridal into a funeral by forgetting their manners; in short, that the thing goes off as well as it can, and that, incidentally, the bridal couple are sent off to get on together as well as they can. But religion, at any rate primitive religion, has an interest of its own in the transaction which cuts deeper than any consideration for the maintenance of social convention. At the very heart of its ritual persists the ancient persuasion that

bride and bridegroom are unclean. They are about
to indulge in relations which tried by the standard of
the primal sanctities are irregular and offensive—
which may be more respectable than fornication or
adultery, but are in value immeasurably below the
chastity that abhors incest.

In his chapter on marriage in *Psyche's Task,* Sir
James Frazer, with his usual industry, has amassed
examples of the ill luck associated by primitive
peoples with breaches of marriage-law of every and
any kind; and a careless reader might easily conclude that incest, fornication, and adultery are more
or less on a par as regard the sinfulness imputed by
religion to all alike. This is by no means actually
the fact, however, as would have been made clearer
if it had been part of the author's plan to consider
likewise the exceptions to the rule, the instances—
and they are numerous—that tell exactly the other
way. Thus incest, it would turn out, is the sin of sins,
and is therefore tolerated only under the most exceptional conditions. Some reference to the matter has
been made already; and, by way of further illustra-
tion, I would merely cite one highly significant fact
taken from the chapter in question. Junod reports
of the Ba-Thonga of South-East Africa that a hippo-
potamus hunter will sometimes commit incest with
his own daughter in order to obtain power over the
game. He thus reckons to become equivalent to a
murderer; a perverse association of ideas assuring
him that the deadliness imparted by deadly sin will

be his by reason of his abominable act. On the other hand, an endless array of proofs would be forthcoming that adultery and fornication are within certain prescribed limits, as in the cases of wife-lending and pre-marital intercourse respectively, normal institutions of primitive society, as if in themselves they involved no taint, but were good or bad according to the circumstances. In any case it is mostly a matter of convention one way or the other, religion lending its support to this policy or that with a smug air of official indifference. Adultery and fornication, within certain limits laid down by the law, are wrongful acts, civil or it may be criminal, variously involving damages, the rod, or even the executioner's knife, as current procedure requires. But in rare cases, if at all, do they excite horror. They are not held to pollute the entire community. They do not smite the people like a plague and the land like a murrain. Incest and the shedding of kinly blood together with witchcraft—these alone are the three deadly sins, as proclaimed by religion from ancient days, long before lawyers or lawyer-like priests had fussed their way into existence.

It remains to examine how far, when the physiology of generation came gradually to be understood, the vastly increased significance attaching to sexual relations made itself correspondingly felt within the religious sphere. Doubtless men always wanted their womenfolk to have plenty of children, even when it was supposed that these came more or less of themselves. Thus the Australians, proceeding on the general principle that all nature, including human nature, can be stimulated to increased fecundity by appropriate rites—rites which should mimetically explain what was wanted, rather than how the want could be supplied—devoted themselves to the metaphysics of child-production, though the physics remained entirely beyond them. One cannot help suspecting that the women, whose department had entire charge of the practical arrangements from the first signs of pregnancy onwards, may have whispered secrets to their daughters that were never passed on to the superior and more enlightened sex. Be this as it may, it is certain that in Australia father-right had been established before any implication of consanguinity attached to the idea of fatherhood in the male mind; while it is likely on the other hand that, from the establishment of father-right onwards, if not before, male influence greatly predominated over female in the shaping of religion. Sir James Frazer indeed has in oracular vein announced: 'Men make the gods and women worship them.' If gods are meant here to include goddesses, he must have made her not so much creatively as cringingly, by accepting motherhood as a mystery in which he could share only from without. Having assisted, however passively, in giving religion this turn from the start, he could not, even with the help of the social revolution that made him master in his own house, reverse the doctrine that, inasmuch as the

blood is the life, it is woman who is the life-giver.
Man's part could only be to furnish something else,
the need of which is not so crassly obvious—something immaterial and subtle, *mana*—the spiritual, as
opposed to the physical, basis of any life worth having. At this point, then, religion was brought to a
parting of the ways, and man, henceforth the pre-
dominant partner, worshipped *mana,* his own contribution to life, while woman was left on the down
grade to worship her contribution, the cruder side of
things as revealed in the experience of childbed and
the nursery. Nay, were it not for the accidental association which brought child-bearing and agriculture
together as alike the woman's affair, the status of the
fertility cult might have sunk even lower than it did.
As it was, when plough-culture superseded hoe-
culture, and for this or some other reason men began
to work the fields by the side of their womenfolk, it
was the latter who were authorities on questions of
birth and growth as viewed from the mystic side; so
that, orgiastic or not, their kind of religion had to this
extent to be allowed full headway. But, as regards
other most important matters, such as notably government and law, male religion kept clear of woman and
woman's religion, as if they were equally unclean. To
woman the things of the body, to man the things of
the soul—such was the principle involved in the division of spiritual labour henceforth approved by the
male mind. The mother-goddess whose kingdom was
of flesh and blood was dethroned. In her place

reigned a father-god, who was fatherly hardly in a procreative sense at all, but on the other hand had all the moral attributes of the *pater familias*—strength, will-power, wisdom, and, most comprehensive gift of all, authority.

For the rest, male experience had discovered the value of training, and the ancient shyness of woman took on a new meaning when it was discovered that continence—the denial of the flesh—was salutarily conducive to the attainment of *mana*. To push such a view to its extreme was not to be expected of the layman, who by this time was fully aware of his physiological share in the raising of the family that he so much desired. The ascetic, on the other hand, who accepted complete celibacy as a necessary part of his task of acquiring spirituality in its absolute form, was doing nothing to offend the male conscience, but on the contrary seemed nearer than the rest to the realization in himself of the perfect man. As by parity of reasoning the same conception should apply to the perfect woman, a spiritual eugenics might seem in prospect that must promptly terminate the earthly career of our ill-starred race. Fortunately the common sense of mankind can distinguish between lust and love; and, without much help from religion, romantic love has fashioned a beautiful out of a purely carnal relation without unreasonably curtailing the rights of nature. Even so, however, human religion can perhaps be excused, nay justified, for the extreme line that it has preferred to take. Paradoxical as it might appear, the life-feeling must by deliberate exaggeration be intensified in the opposite direction to the all-powerful trend of the reproductive instinct, if, instead of merely living, man seriously desires to live well. Sexual passion, as Plato says, is a madness. At the animal level it recklessly flings out offspring, mostly to perish prematurely. At the human level, however, although it may have been almost as prodigal of cheap life in the earliest days, it was gradually reduced to sanity by a remedial process that as it were decentralized the madness—spread it out through the entire man, so that instead of bodily lust there could be a spiritual lustiness, a divine madness, an infinite passion to engender all things good.

V

CRUELTY

Hunting as the earliest mystery-craft must have helped to invest blood with a sacredness that may account for the origin of cooking as a purificatory rite; while the slaying of the animal, wild or domesticated, is felt to need apology. So too in human sacrifice, the victim, slave or enemy though he be, is never without a certain sacredness, which extending also to the slain criminal, transforms each into a kind of martyr, as is more obviously the case with the king slain at the end of his term of office, or the widow who undergoes suttee. These, then, vicariously represent a general habit of self-torture which, though sublimated into self-sacrifice, looks back to ugly beginnings.

AMONG the natural stimulants to which human emotion is more especially susceptible is blood of any description. Just as the smell or taste of it will drive certain animals almost frantic either with the presage of death or with the killing fever, so any kind of sensible contact with it, including the bare sight, is enough to cause the primitive kind of man to lose his mental balance. Anything, in fact, from complete nausea to a wild exhilaration may result from the violent fluctuation of his feelings. Now the one extreme case was perhaps sufficiently illustrated by the incest-taboo with which we dealt last time; for there can be little doubt that, however it may have come about, the horror of incest is with the savage essentially the horror of sinning against the blood. With the other extreme case it remains to deal in the present lecture. A certain craving for bloodshed is a feature of the cruder forms of religion which, however revolting, we cannot ignore, if we are seeking to understand their psychological sources, or indeed if we should wish to account on historical lines for various survivals and sublimations that are to be found in civilized religion taken at its highest. Not that outbursts of the blood-lust pure and simple are likely to be encountered within the religious sphere. There is always something mixed—something, as Freud would say, ambivalent—about emotion in its specifically religious character that lends to its clearest note an overtone of discord; so that life-feeling is modified by death-feeling, hope by fear, to the fuller enrichment of the whole affective quality and significance. Thus the worst kind of religious cruelty is never quite merciless, even when the sympathy shown with the suffering inflicted is little more than a disguised self-pity. Given the necessary state of exaltation, the slaying of a human being or even of an animal takes on a note of tragedy, as if each participant were privy to a death that might as well be his own; and this suggestion of danger is never quite overcome, even when the pendulum swings towards joy, and the particular death is regarded as affording ransom or positive provision for a life universal.

Let us begin by imagining the human hunting-pack of the remotest pre-Palaeolithic era—men or half-men who have acquired a taste for flesh and are fairly adept at getting it, but have yet to learn the use of fire. For such folk both killing and eating will be a bloody business, and the one will follow on the other so closely that there will be little time, if plenty of reason, for saying grace. Wolfishly they will tear and mangle their prey, licking their own wounds by way of a dessert. Give them what credit we can for a nascent humanity that would put them a degree ahead of the real wolf-pack in their table manners— let them for example be already too well-disciplined to squabble seriously over the pickings—even so it could not have been a pretty sight. For the matter of that the modern Eskimo, so advanced, if perhaps one can hardly say so refined, in their cultural habits, yet are reported to get inside a stranded whale as a preliminary to getting outside it, and literally no less than metaphorically to soak themselves in blubber. Or, again, every African traveller knows that his native escort, however keen and efficient they may be, cannot be moved from fresh meat that he has shot for them until every scrap has been blissfully swallowed by gormandizers for whom surfeit has no meaning. Poets must have sung of food long before they sang of drink—so long ago, in fact, that no surviving literature does justice to the primitive notion of a feast, not even Homer or Rabelais. Eating was life renewed, life glorified; and since it was an eating together—for the first law of the human pack must have been to insist on that—it was the social life that was renewed in glory. If communion needed a symbol, here it was.

Now the blood which in those early days we may suppose to have been equally in evidence in the killing and the eating might well seem to be the central principle of the joint transaction—the pivot on which the feelings of each and all swung round from fear to hope, from the threat of starvation to the promise of replenished strength. Whenever kill-to-eat became a mystery, blood was palpably the heart of it. Meanwhile, hunting is essentially a mystery-craft—the earliest of a long series. As the game is unaccountable in its ways, even so must the hunter be circumspect in his. He must be void of offence in the eyes of the beasts, so quick to notice as they are and so ready to take umbrage. That they have to be killed and eaten is clear; it is what they are for. No reasonable beast, then, ought to object if the thing is done properly, that is, with all the respect due to his natural feelings. Now in times of dearth, when the game was scarce and shy, it might strike the group-elders, hungrily and therefore pensively contrasting their present lot with former seasons of prosperity, that possibly they had been somewhat too lavish in their killing. They would almost certainly not reason it out that they had drawn too heavily on stock. Yet, with a far dimmer sense of cause and effect, they might go so far as to conclude that somehow they had made the beasts angry. Unholy orgies of slaughter might come back to mind from those lost, nay, forfeited, days of superabundance. Thus at Solutré, not far from Lyons, there is a veritable Golgotha, composed of horses', and mostly of young horses', bones, where the hunters of the Late Palaeolithic must evidently have held high and wasteful revel. From the position of this vast bone-heap, at the foot of an abrupt escarpment, it has been inferred that the wild horses were corralled and driven over the edge *en masse* by encircling tactics similar to those which the Plains Indians of North America used on the bison with exactly the same object and result. What a wild slaughter must have gone on among the foundered and struggling brutes, and, despite prodigies of carnivoracity, what fat leavings must have remained for the vultures and hyenas! I recollect how, because a white man in Australia had poisoned a wombat for burrowing in his garden, a native was horrified and said to me most solemnly of the waster of food, 'him bad fellow'. I can easily conceive, then, how to the conscience of the ancient hunter there might come pangs sympathetic with those of his belly and charged with protest against his former extravagance. Somehow, then, he must propitiate the injured beasts by denying himself. He must answer for too greedy a killing by eating less greedily. To atone for bloodshed he must taboo blood.

Anthropologists are wont to explain the origin of cooking on the principle of Charles Lamb's story of how the Chinaman discovered the virtues of roast pork. They suppose that having started a fire, or having merely come across one, in which something succulent had been done to a turn, man started his career as an epicure, forswearing omophagy from that moment on. I venture to suggest, however, that the culinary art may have had its source in religion, the original object being to purify the meat—to cleanse it from the taint of blood. Indeed, fire itself may from the first have belonged to the category of sacred things; in which case the power imputed to it might well have been chiefly of a destructive order, before closer acquaintance had revealed the kindly side of its nature. Howsoever this may be, blood-drinking and the eating of raw meat are in later times associated with Dionysiac rites and similar outbursts of orgiastic frenzy. From religious licence one can usually infer a religious prohibition in the opposite sense holding for normal as contrasted with exceptional and abnormal occasions. For the rest, if blood-less eating was not adopted simply and wholly as an atonement for bloodshed, there was an additional reason of a kind convincing to the savage intelligence why the blood should not be consumed, namely, that it must be restored if the game was to be made to live again. Every hunter, thanks to what Tylor calls his butcher's anatomy, would know that the heart with the heart's blood is the stronghold of the life of his prize, the bull's eye of his target. The artists of the French and Spanish caves make this clear by painting a large red heart just where it ought to be found in the animals that figure in their pictured incantations. Hence it would be good policy, if the game is to be helped to reincarnate in due course, to send the blood, that is the life, back thither whence it came. However, then, it may have happened, the blood of the slain animal became holy, a thing most dangerous, yet pregnant with the hope of good hunting and of good fortune in general. All men believed that, if dealt with religiously and in due form, it was no less instinct with blessing for the wise than, used profanely, it was fraught with bane for the foolish.

Passing on to conditions which come more directly under observation, we have next to note that, by way of apology for liberties taken in the ordinary course of doing an animal-kind to death, it became the practice to kill ritually a representative of the kind in question in order to show that mankind appreciated the delicacy of the situation—that, in short, the intentions of the hunter were nice, even if his proceedings were at times inevitably nasty. Numerous instances of propitiatory ceremonies of this class could be cited both as associated with totemism and apart from any such complicating condition. Of the latter variety a typical example is the bear-feast of the Ainu, which has parallels among the Palaeo-Siberian tribes with whom the Ainu have affinities in the way of culture if not of blood. The facts are too well known to need detailed description. Suffice it to say, that a young bear is first loaded with favours and then treated to the happy dispatch, so that he may in due course be born again, and in the meantime may inform the other bears how much the Ainu love them in the most comprehensive sense of the word. The sufferer resumes the universal, if hardly divine, nature that is in him as a bear, while as the messenger of mankind he confesses their faults and conveys their desire for forgiveness. As for man himself, he cannot or at any rate will not forgo his career as a man of blood; yet, by the paradoxical means of an additional act of cruelty, he repents of his natural propensity to kill. By bringing a certain regret, half sham half real, to bear on it, he gives rise within himself to a more complex mood of sympathy with all life, including the life on which his animal nature forces him to prey. A beast may slay ruthlessly, but not a man. Even the gory symbolism of the hunter—the mere food-seeker who is not yet a food-raiser—suggests that the human, as propelled by a heightened stir of the life-feeling, is already bound in the direction of the humane.

When the food-raiser has come to his own and animals have become domesticated, the ritual slaying of them continues with little change of meaning; for training and humouring are parts of one process, and it was doubtless by treating the beast more or less as if he were a man, and so giving him the full benefit of any doubts that there might be about it, that eventually certain animal-kinds—not many of them, it is true, but so many as they amount to of immeasurable

value to mankind—were half forced and half induced to enter man's service. Not having yet
acquired the outlook of the complete slave-driver,
the savage is apt to look upon the domesticated
animal as a friend and, indeed, as the word domestication implies, as part of his household, as a member
of his family. Killing to eat in such circumstances
could be little better than an act of endo-cannibalism; though to a savage this would not necessarily
mean that it was therefore an impious thing to do.
What is known to anthropologists as senicide, the
putting away of elderly relatives who have become
useless mouths, or who cannot stand the hardships of
the trail, can be shown to have formerly been a fairly
common custom with primitive peoples, whether
they were driven to it by an invincible necessity, or
had succumbed to baser motives such as the love of
ease. In any such case, however, they would be sure
to acknowledge the pathos of the situation by ex-
plaining away the death as some sort of happy release
—as a departure, however premature, to some gather-
ing of the clan, some reunion of the family. So, too,
then, the domestic animal, if slain and eaten—for,
however edible, he will often be allowed by primitive folk to live out his life in peace—must be ac-
corded something like funeral honours. The women,
for example, will be expected to set up a loud lament,
as they do among the Dinka on such an occasion.
The theory that the victim is going back to be reborn
may by this time have faded almost away; but even

so the animal-kind is held to retain a collective interest in the affair. Hence, if the cattle go wrong in a body, man knows that he has done something to offend them—has seethed the kid in its mother's milk, or has otherwise sinned against the proprieties. Thus, however lacking in divinity the animal-kind may have become, supposing that at any time it possessed it—and the so-called divinity of the totem may easily be rated far too high—the act of shedding his blood is likely to retain a religious quality. Always it remains the act of a butcher-priest—one who slays solemnly, because he inflicts death not for its own sake but for the sake of further life.

Before discussing the subject of the slaying of animals, let us also remember that, apart from those which provide food, or, though not normally eaten, like the dog, are otherwise useful, there are destructive beasts, the sworn foes of the human race. Thus on the whole the felidae proudly defy man's efforts to dominate them, though the cheetah may condescend to hunt with him rather than for him, and the cat with ill-disguised contempt has allowed itself to descend into domesticity by way of deification; while, for the rest, the flesh of one and all is anything but toothsome. Here, then, it might seem was from man's point of view a case for relentless slaughter. How could any sentiment stand in the way of the annihilation of the public enemy? Yet, as man knew to his cost, the purely noxious beast was brave, even uncannily so; he might, in fact, be trusted to put up a very 'devil' of a fight. Thus a grudging respect mingled with the hate that he inspired. Partly to conciliate him, partly to acquire his death-dealing qualities, one might eat a portion of him sacramentally, despite the protest of the stomach; or, more conveniently, especially if the object were to borrow his fearsomeness, one could add his claws to one's armoury of war-charms, or make other use of the remains of such a spiritual ally. Nay, a leopard-society might be formed to assimilate his qualities, even though his man-eating proclivities must be imitated in order to become the perfect leopard-man. At the same time, if the strongest kind of killing *mana* could thus be acquired, the taboo on eating the flesh in a common and profane way must be proportionately strict. Religion would second nature in proclaiming this to be the very type of an unclean meat—something that on ordinary occasions must be put beyond the risk of harm by calling in the aid of the very elements—consigning to the unclean birds of the air, burying in earth, drowning in water, or, most effective riddance of all, purging by the sacred agency of fire. Thus even the killing of the devil-beast generated an emotion that played double—roused a hate and relieved a fear, both of them tinged alike with admiration for a power which, duly modified, a man would gladly have for himself.

Passing on from the butchery of animals to the far more sinister butchery of human beings, it is fortunate that man-slaying is on the whole too dangerous a business—one too likely to prove a case of catching a Tartar—to have ever made it possible to solve the economic problem on cannibalistic lines. Being perfectly nutritious, human flesh may have quite occasionally become an article, even a prized article, of diet in regions, such as Oceania or parts of Africa, where meat was otherwise difficult to obtain. On the whole, however, this may be treated as an exceptional and morbid development of society, and we may therefore expect to find no general analogy between manslaughter and the killing of animals, wild or tame, for food. In such a connexion, however, it is worth observing that, whenever ritual homicide displays, as it sometimes does, a tendency to be reck-lessly prodigal of human life, it is precisely at that stage of society at which a domesticated animal has been made out of man by the institution of slavery. It may easily come to be felt among the class of the dominants that, if a blood-sacrifice is needed, a human drudge will answer the purpose as well as or better than an animal drudge. Nay, as the psychology of the man is better understood than that of the brute, it might even seem that less harm was likely to ensue from offending so powerless a kind of creature as a slave than from giving reason, let us say, to a cow to go off her milk. Though it is easier to prove that animal victims have been substituted for human than that the opposite process has occurred, it may well be that the latter possibility has also to be reckoned with. It must be added that the slave, who is perfectly aware that he will be sacrificed one day, even when treated kindly in the meantime and perhaps encouraged to raise a family with the same grim destiny in prospect, is apt to show all the meek unconcern of the unthinking cattle. One certainly cannot attribute to him what Matthew Arnold has termed, in a mood that must have been a racial inheritance from Old Testament days, 'the blood-thirsty love of life of the British middle-classes'. Yet any human worm will turn, and it is refreshing to hear from Livingstone's lips how he once met a slave-gang who, with the African's readiness to look at the brighter side of things, were chanting as they went of what plagues they would inflict on their captors as soon as they were ghosts. And, truly, whatever curse might be brewing for their oppressors would be well deserved!

The dangerous animal, then, rather than the domesticated one, must provide the parallel when we consider that typical form of human sacrifice in which the victim is a public enemy, whether foreigner or native. Thus, to deal first with the member of a rival group, he is at the least that wicked kind of beast which defends itself when attacked, and for the matter of that his greed or even his fear may at any time prompt him to play the aggressor. In the world's central areas of competition the pressure of population in itself makes it necessary for each people to choose between being hammer or anvil; so that to hate the enemy and to survive become almost convertible terms. To keep up one's courage—always an uncertain quality in a man, in whom a cold-blooded ferocity is not normal, and at most is second nature, a matter of training—all sorts of devices must be used, moral no less than technical; and primitive religion cannot be wholly blamed if it gives its blessing to the war-dance. Even in Australia, with nothing to steal except women, with plenty of room for all, and with no dangerous animals to excite the hunter to fury, we learn from Howitt that the Kurnai of Gippsland made a point not only of slaying the *brajerak* or strange black, but of ceremonially eating a portion of him; reserving another portion for the youths left behind in camp, that they should likewise eat and know what to do when their turn came. I may mention by the way that wishing to recommend myself to an old Kurnai woman, almost the last of her race, by showing some knowledge of her language, I referred to myself as a *brajerak* with most unfortunate results, as the old lady shook with contemptuous laughter at the expense of one who by his own confession was a barbarian, a foreign devil. Nowhere, however, has the torturing and ritual slaying of the war-captive been carried to such pitiless lengths as on the American Continent, and notably by the most civilized of the indigenous stocks. It is almost as if the natural stoicism of the redskin temperament demanded unusual effort on the part of those who would wear it down to breaking-point. There may be some exaggeration in the accounts which the old Spanish writers have left of atrocities in the way of human

sacrifice from all the advanced peoples of Central
and South America alike; but the Mexican war-god
undoubtedly accounted for more victims than even
the Spanish Inquisition that took his place. Nowhere else does one hear of expeditions conducted
with the simple object of collecting pabulum for the
altar; and there is reason to think that the Mexicans
themselves, whose moral standards were so high in
other respects, were becoming heartily sick of a custom which from no possible point of view was anything but disgusting. It made it little better that here
as elsewhere in a continent which was deficient in
domesticable animals human sacrifice had come to
be adopted as a general means of obtaining the favour
of the gods; as, for instance, when the maize-goddess
was propitiated with rites that put a somewhat different complexion on the victim's character, so that he
seemed rather mediator than scapegoat. Yet, whatever the gloss put upon it, there was cruelty, intensified by cult into *mania sanguinis,* behind the most
developed religion of native America. For the rest,
however well one searches the whole primitive world
for instances in which ritual proceedings reflect admiration for the virtues of the slain enemy mingled
with the hate that is the primary reaction towards
him, very little that is edifying comes to light, while
there is much to illustrate the text, *homo homini
lupus.*

That the execution of the criminal can be brought
under the head of sacrifice might seem, from the

standpoint of modern law, absurd, though a careful study of the confusion of ideas underlying the legal theory of punishment might suggest that it depends to this day far less on rational than on emotional considerations. Every punishment is a public protest of a spectacular kind against a given type of crime at the expense of the particular criminal; and the blame attaching to him in this vicarious character overshadows such personal guilt as helps to justify his fate. When we go back to primitive peoples we find little attention paid to individual desert, or indeed to the voluntary aspect of the offence at all; and this is especially true of that major kind of wrongdoing which consists in the violation of a taboo. In the case of such a crime, or rather sin, the offender is as it were slain by his own act, and society merely intervenes to remove the body, bearing witness meanwhile to the judgement of God. Afterwards, every one can breathe again because something unclean has been removed from the midst of the assembly. Pitied for his misfortune rather than hated for his transgression, the vessel of wrath is cast away: SACER ESTO, let him be accurst. In his miserable person the majesty of the Divine dispensation so vindicates itself that all may see and be aware. Unwilling as any victim in his private capacity is bound to be, the sufferer nevertheless dies to save others. Feared for his malevolence, yet prized for his unwitting beneficence, he acquires a *mana* which renders him redoubtable whether for good or ill; so that any relic of him and especially his blood is potent. The Sicilian peasant still reckons the *decollati*—decapitated persons of notoriety—as very much on a par with the saints in their power of rewarding suitable attentions. Meanwhile, apart from the incidental blessings which all the world over are deemed to be obtainable by ritual means from the death of the social outcast, there can be little doubt that the blood of the martyrs of superstition is the seed of an effective administration of justice. For instance, Captain Rattray's recent study of Ashanti law makes it clear that in the native view all matters calling for judicial intervention fall into two classes, man-palavers and god-palavers, trivial and serious. The first are settled with a minimum of fuss by the fathers of households. The second alone come under the cognizance of the state, which, however, regards itself as simply the organ and mandatary of a divine justice, which accuser and accused invoke by each calling down a conditional curse on himself if he be in the wrong. The drawback to such a procedure is that there is only one penalty in the serious kind of case, namely death; for the rejected of heaven cannot benefit the earth, except in so far as he purges it by renouncing his life. On the other hand, human authority by claiming and acknowledging a higher sanction than the will of a despot both gains immeasurably in its influence over the minds of men, and interprets its own prerogative in a way likely to convert it into an impersonal instrument of the public welfare.

From criminal to king, from sinner to sacrosanct head of the state, there stretches a social gulf which primitive religion bridges by declaring both alike to be consecrated lives. At this point we find ourselves passing from sacrifice to self-sacrifice, from the unwilling to the willing victim. The animal, the enemy, the offender against the law—all these die wrathfully, like cornered rats. Their slayers, uneasily aware that it is of such stuff that avenging ghosts are made, do their best to propitiate, that is, to cajole them. In Mexico they even went so far as to give the war-captive a chance, tethered as he was to the stone of sacrifice, and furnished only with a wooden sword, to defend himself against fully armed assailants who attacked him in succession; and if he slew four—some authorities say six—of these in turn, the gladiator was spared. On the whole, however, the celebrants show a callous indifference, or even a perverse delight, in regard to the death-pangs of the medium of their edification. The student of the psychology of primitive religion must face the fact that the thrill of the obscene in all its forms can for the time being quicken the sense of life; as if any stirring of the mud was bound to bring up hope together with the rest from the depths of the human soul. Meanwhile, whatever biological justification there may be for the promotion of life at the cost of other life, even when provided from within the same species, it is far easier to discover a moral excuse for it when the sacrifice is voluntary. The most pertinacious stickler for a cosmic justice will hardly deny that there is seemliness or even sweetness in the act of the man who dies for his country. Thus the primitive king, of whose resignation by apotheosis Sir James Frazer has written so much, is hardly to be counted among those royal martyrs who have been murdered judicially or otherwise by their rebellious subjects. The chief of the Shilluk or of Unyoro was from the first aware that he must be slain before old age could impair the *mana* which it was his duty to hand on intact to his successor; and, however fatalistically, acquiesced in the custom and constitution of his country. It is true that the most divine of monarchs has his human side; so that one cannot be surprised if the King of Calicut preferred a ceremony in which the would-be slayer of royalty was cut down so as to provide a victim by substitution; or if a Nubian prince, whose mind had been warped by a civilized education, anticipated his own removal by massacring the entire college of priests, and so ingloriously attained a ripe old age. In the typical and uncontaminated instance, however, the savage ruler whose life is thus dedicated under the terms of his sacred office meets his appointed doom in the spirit of an ancient Roman; and self-sacrifice in an undeveloped form has come into existence to relieve a bloodthirsty superstition of the charge of utter foulness.

Another type of religious, or, one may well say, superstitious, observance in which one can descry the beginnings of self-sacrifice is the Indian suttee, together with similar developments on a grander scale; so that from ancient Sumer to modern Dahomey there come before the mind's eye majestic if gloomy pageants of some mighty despot starting off to the next world with a long retinue of wives and attendants. Those who were actually consentient spectators of such last rites were doubtless moved by pity and fear, yet above all other feelings there must have prevailed sheer admiration for the loyalty thus fittingly displayed; for where else should these others be, or want to be, except beside their lord and master? It may be that the widows of lesser men do not always exhibit the same willingness to share their fate; but their public duty is not so obvious to all, including themselves, nor do they—if it is not unduly cynical to say so—enjoy so public an opportunity of manifesting their devotion. So let custom be made responsible for the needless waste of life, and let the victims have full credit for being faithful unto death. Here again, then, something noble emerges from the association of religion with the blood-lust.

A few concluding words must suffice on the subject of self-sacrifice of the developed type in which the compelling motive clearly comes from within. It would perhaps be vain to search the savage world for a pure case, seeing that the primitive conscience is on the whole unreflective and amounts to little more than a sense of social propriety. On the other hand, it would be a mistake to suppose that the ordinary

member of the community regards himself as exempt
from the obligation to suffer personal hardship
which religious duty enjoins on kings, widows, and
so on, in what might be called their official capacity.
To begin with, these cruelties inflicted on individuals
in virtue of their special status are as it were but refinements of painful experiences to which every one
is liable in the normal course of things. Thus killing
the king is senicide *in excelsis;* or suttee is cutting for
the dead carried a point further. Even the slaying
of the war-captive in Ancient Mexico, which might
seem from the onlooker's point of view as festive an
occasion as the hanging of a highwayman used to be
made in England, involved the ministrations of
priests who resorted to every means of self-torture,
from piercing their tongues with the sharp spines of
the aloe to complete self-mutilation; while on various
solemn occasions the rest of the worshippers, male
and female, would cut themselves freely in order to
make blood-offerings to their cannibal gods. It
would indeed be easy to cite examples from every
part of America, not to speak of the remaining con-
tinents, of penitential practices which if directed towards others would have to be stigmatized as cruel
in the extreme. Such scarifications and skewerings
as, for instance, the Plains Indians inflicted on themselves may have been partly intended as tests of endurance, means of obtaining ecstatic experiences, and
so on; but in the main their object was primarily to
excite pity by their sufferings and loud laments, even

when it remained obscure whose pity was sought. From the human end it was enough to know that thus to mortify the flesh made strong medicine. Now there is a well-known type of neurotic who appears to enjoy the taste of pain, and paradoxical, as it may sound, such a mania for self-torture is to be treated as a development of the blood-lust. The wretched fakir who chews glass is psychologically not far removed from the Grand Inquisitor; and seeing that, as compared with the hunter or the warrior, the priest has less excuse to be a man of blood, it is perhaps poetic justice that, if he is to shed blood at all, it should be his own.

It may be, then, that in the eyes of the psychologist no less than in those of the historian of religion the notion of self-sacrifice must always have a suspect air. Courage and endurance are noble virtues, but they can be associated with hope no less easily than with suffering; and, though a remedial value may undoubtedly attach to suffering in the sense that it may be unavoidable during the process of recovery, the suffering as such is of no use in itself, and does not even afford a test of the efficacy of the cure. Thanks to the grosser forms of the sacrificial rite, the middle religions—not those of savages so much as those of the half-civilized peoples—reek of blood like a shambles. It was the sacrifice of Iphigeneia that called forth the protest of Lucretius in immortal verse: *tantum religio potuit suadere malorum.* Yet if the facts are so, let us face them fairly. If religion is liable to unloose the beast in us even while seeking to free the man, we must learn how this deviation occurs, so that religion may be kept to the true direction. As psychologists, then, we must not be content to speak together in whispers about the lust or the cruelty that found their way into the religious complex together with the noblest of the human tendencies. Let us honestly proclaim that religious emotion is ambivalent, exciting the mind at once for better and for worse. At times, then, man is apt to think that he has reached the heights when he has merely touched the lowest depths of his spiritual nature.

VI

FAITH

It is not inconsistent with the hopefulness inherent in primitive religion that it should rest on a faith in tradition, though this might seem to contradict the tendency of the immature mind to indulge in random play. Another trait of such a mind being to enjoy repetition by rote, it is on this that the static type of society seizes in order to obtain the rigid system of law that it needs. The cyclical view of life, reflected in the belief in reincarnation, implies a round of duties comprised in a sacred custom, and only faith in its infallibility can supply the moral effort needed to maintain it.

IN one of the profoundest, if not the least paradoxical, of his essays, entitled *Youth and Crabbed Age,* Robert Louis Stevenson does his best to turn the tables on the solemn elder who, in the name of authority, rebukes the rising generation for its irresponsible doings and wild opinions. For no revelation, he argues, comes with the passing of the years. We merely suffer a change of mood; so that what felt at the time like an 'undying hope' is replaced by an 'infallible credulity' which we proceed to mistake in ourselves for a ripened wisdom. These settled convictions, however, in which we take such pride, are

perhaps not due to growth of experience so much as
to decline of animal heat. Because we have lost the
taste for living dangerously, it does not follow that
we have reached safety. 'A man finds he has been
wrong at every preceding stage of his career, only to
deduce the astonishing conclusion that he is at last
entirely right.' Yet in reality such a dull respectable
person is no sage. He provides, indeed, the veriest
parody of an angel because he has finally shed his
wings. He has joined the ranks of those who 'take
everything as it comes in a forlorn stupidity'—who
'swallow the universe like a pill'. But thus to claim
enlightenment as one's portion is simply to have
given up trying to transform for the better a defective
world which includes the existing moral outlook of
a man and the present state of his knowledge. Any
advance implies a method of trial and error. In fact,
'all error, not merely verbal, is a strong way of stating
that the current truth is incomplete'. Hence human
perfectibility would seem to depend more on the experiments of the sons than on the dogmas of the
fathers. For, after all, 'it is better to be a fool than
to be dead'—or even dead-alive. Wherefore Stevenson, the sick man whose body denied him the adventures for which his soul craved, cries out: 'For God's
sake, give me the young man who has brains enough
to make a fool of himself!'

Now savagery is commonly held to bear a certain
analogy to the adolescence of the human race. If,
therefore, Stevenson is right in his psychology, un-

dying hope should prove to be its dominant mood, while 'infallible credulity' ought as yet to have had no chance to develop. On such a theory of the youth of the world, prehistory might be expected to provide us with the spectacle of gay, go-ahead peoples, heroically intent on taking time by the forelock, and not afraid of playing the fool. It turns out, however, that only on a very long view of the progress of mankind can a case be made out for that innate hopefulness which must have been there all along as a prime mover. Nay, the immense sluggishness of cultural evolution in its earlier stages would almost seem to justify a Platonic myth to the effect that, racially speaking, Man was born an ancient, but is visibly growing younger every day. Thus a cave-man might well be pardoned for thinking modern America, or even Great Britain, raw and childish. For he knew the difference between the right and the wrong way of doing things down to the last touch to the edge of a flint-knife; whereas our standards are as various as the wares of a toy-shop. Or, again, he was content to take his cue from his tribal elders; whereas our manners and even our morals are at the mercy of 'the younger set'. In short, the cave-man, like any other savage, prided himself on being the acme of respectability. Yet Stevenson's biting phrase 'infallible credulity' reminds us that adherence to fixed principles has its weak side. It remains to take stock of the advantages and the drawbacks of living by rule a little more precisely.

To begin with, it may be observed that a policy of going slow finds favour with every other animal species except our own, and is a mark of the predominance of instinct. Now instinct is a tyrant, while its chief minister, habit, is even more insistent on passive obedience in the subject organism. Nevertheless there is a reason in the life of the higher type of animal when it is allowed a taste of freedom. Play may be only Nature's way of disguising school-discipline, but on the face of it the activity seems to be markedly autonomous, partly because there is a superabundance of energy ready to be let loose at random, and partly because the unimportance of the objects on which it is exercised does away with the need of caution and self-restraint. So too, then, the savage has his full share of play during childhood, and enjoys it all the more thoroughly because superintendence on the part of his elders is notoriously slack. For better or worse, the primitive community allows its progeny to grow up wild; though it should be noted that 'wild' in this context only means 'at will', and by no means implies an innate tendency to grow up crooked. Spontaneous imitation furnishes no bad substitute for the elementary school. Although Dame Nature lacks the adventitious support of spectacles and birch, she manages to keep her class at once busy and amused. Call it what we will—nature, instinct, the unconscious—something of racial origin and import stirs in every childish bosom which urges on the youngster to forestall destiny by rehearsing with the zest of a born actor his future part on the world's stage. Thanks to a sort of active dreaming, the bud figures itself as the full-blown flower, and thereby positively determines its own unfolding.

Now have we not here, in the play of children, the natural prototype and model of all those symbolisms whereby mankind has sought to envisage the ideal? Just as the ambition of youth, as revealed in play, is to anticipate its own development by feigning to have already taken the step that lies ahead, so the whole cultural process may be said to be actuated by the will to pretend that we are grown-up and in the full enjoyment of our manhood, when in point of fact we are nothing of the kind. To realize the human potential in vision, however fleeting and unsubstantial, is the preoccupation of those choicer spirits who are in the forefront of the human host. These lead on none the less surely because their methods are more akin to those of the medicine-man than to those of the war-chief. Childlike enough to enjoy the drama, not to say the conjuring, for its own sake, they so impose on themselves and on the rest as to cause their fancy to pass as fact, their will for the very deed. There can be no lying down in peace for such a 'hunter home from the hill', since he would rather dance under the moon and make big magic in aid of tomorrow's adventure.

Even so, however, though we make full allowance for the workings of that spirit of play which appeals to the *Ewigkindliches* in us all, we must not forget that such progress as our species can be said to have accomplished is incidental to a process which consists largely in sheer repetition. Indeed, when the child plays at being the man, he does not evince the slightest conscious desire to improve on the authorized version of the part. If he reads into it anything new, he does it unwittingly, and because he himself is a new creature—not a chip from a dead block, but a slip from a living stem which can impart the power of living afresh and independently. Thus the old Adam was reproduced in Cain and Abel with considerable difference in each case. Doubtless the causes of variation in Man or in any other organic stock remain exceedingly obscure and in large measure defy control; but one might guess that the sheer multiplication of the human family has greatly increased variability and with it the rate of change in respect to social customs of all kinds. Be this so or not, the normal child displays conformity to type in the highest degree—a tendency which on its mental side can almost be equated with herd-feeling. Never are we more gregariously disposed than in childhood; and this sheeplike habit in itself is bound to suppress all inclination to diverge. Further, the economy of individual growth would seem to demand of the tiro a certain mechanization of elementary functions by continuous exercise—a sort of practising of scales—which carries with it little or no sense of monotony so long as the appropriate age-limit is not exceeded. Explain it, then, as we may, conservatism rules in the nursery, and the child is the foremost, because the most single-minded, champion and exponent of that time-honoured faith. Alter one word of his favourite story, and he protests. On the other hand, the greatest compliment that he can pay to our efforts to entertain him is to shout, 'Again!' It does not follow, therefore, because savage childhood, though all too short, is relatively untrammelled while it lasts, that it interprets its freedom as a freedom to differ. Indiscipline there may be, but it does not breed unorthodoxy. The child at play proves to be an impersonator who revels in stock characters, very much as happens with the rustic when he engages in folk-drama. In short, the immature mind is conventional even in its make-believe. Indeed in modern education it is all too easy to produce a cheap and commonplace uniformity by trading on this juvenile propensity to repeat by rote and according to some set fashion; whereas the more difficult task is usually shirked of bringing out that infinitely more precious originality of which all have a few grains hidden within them, while here and there an industrious prospector may expect to strike some richer vein.

In the next place, let us consider why childhood under the conditions of primitive existence is bound to be brief, nay, unduly curtailed. Truly it might be said of the young savage who undergoes initiation on reaching puberty that

> Shades of the prison-house begin to close
> Upon the growing boy.

Essentially initiation is a preparation for marriage, and, although it may sound cynical to say so, when a man marries in the hard, hand-to-mouth world of typical savagery, his troubles begin. The same, of course, holds equally of the woman, whose lot as the child-bearer is perhaps even harder, though Nature has a way of adjusting the weight of the yoke to each kind of neck in bearable proportion. As for the burdensome nature of the social, and more especially the economic, responsibilities attendant on such early matrimony, tending as they do to bear most heavily on juniors, partly because of their inexperience but chiefly in consequence of the inferiority of their tribal status, one has only to consult Miss Margaret Mead's incisive sketch entitled *Growing up in New Guinea*. Family and fun are here shown to be incompatible on evidence that can hardly be gainsaid, unless it were by arguing that, since happiness is largely a matter of standards, there is less weariness of such tough flesh than a civilized observer might suppose. Not to dwell further on this particular point, which is, however, of primary importance inasmuch as a faculty of rapid reproduction is the *sine qua non* of survival at this level of society, let us go on to note how, apart from its function as a finishing school for those about to marry, initiation is largely concerned with teaching the young idea how not to shoot in undesirable directions. Its Spartan method of testing manhood by the infliction of pain on the pretext of circumcision, knocking out a tooth, or other ritual purpose reveals a policy of the heavy hand which must be all the more daunting to the novice because, as we have seen, he has hitherto been mostly left to his own devices. His passport to the new life is some outrage wrought on his person. Ere he can make good his entrance he must be branded as fit for social service. He will be admitted into the order of the adult only when he can show the stigmata of what is veritably a consecration. His vow to be a true man must have been sealed with his own blood.

Now what is the moral to be drawn from the severities common to so many savage initiations? For such facts can be matched from all the greater areas of characterization, Australia, America, Africa; though it may be that more easy-going ways are reported of sheltered peoples, whether they are so situated that they can exploit a geographical isolation, or simply have softened and grown listless under the *Pax Britannica.* Surely the implication of the harsh treatment meted out to impressionable youth is that they must be taught to accommodate themselves to authority in the form of a system of the sternest repressions. Such negative prescriptions must ever abound in a law which, like that of the Medes and Persians, 'altereth not'. Every savage could subscribe to the Pythagorean maxim that there is only one way of doing right as against infinite ways of doing wrong. Kipling's jingle about the 'nine and sixty ways of constructing tribal lays' is, on the contrary, more in harmony with the spirit of the modern world; for 'where no law is, there is no transgression', and, where no dogma is, there can be no persecution. In an age of conscious experimentation, so long as each is prepared to stand by his own mistakes, he has usually no difficulty in obtaining his letters of marque from the guardians of the public. But the old-world name for an experimenter is 'pirate'. Liberty is identified with libertinism, and neither the one nor the other can be enjoyed under official charter so long as Custom is king. It is no doubt accidental that in Latin the same word *codex* should stand indifferently for a whipping-post, a blockhead, and the book of the law; but by punning in the decent obscurity of a dead language one might make a trope of it to express in one 'portmanteau word' the triple aim of the primitive legislator as regards educational machinery, mental product, and social pattern. To codify sums up the ideal of the *ancien régime*.

Now it might seem a paradox to maintain that in what Herbert Spencer would describe as the static as contrasted with the dynamic type of human society there is provided just as ample an opportunity for living strenuously, or, if we like to recur to Stevenson's phrase, for living dangerously. Indeed, of the two, the savage and the civilized man, it is undubitably the former who runs the greater risk of sudden extinction, whether individual or collective. If we be inclined to award ourselves the palm on the strength of the record-breaking efforts of our speed-mongers and high-fliers, in whose feats the majority of us participate with the help of an evening-paper and an easy chair, we need only purge our pride with a dose of vital statistics. It will thereupon appear that effectively, if in less spectacular fashion, the chances of death weigh heavily against the humdrum folk who hunt and fish and scratch for roots and collect firewood among snakes and sharks and crocodiles and lions—not to mention next-door neighbours with head-hunting or cannibal tastes. Thus it is easy to underrate the mild excitements of the simple life. Stevenson himself might have composed an essay on 'living dangerously in Samoa' to remind himself that hoary age can plead justification under primitive conditions for not courting a danger which is ever present and in act to claim fresh victims. It is no discredit to the hardiest mariner that he should reef his sails in a storm. Indeed, to drift under bare poles was about the only thing to be done on such a sea of troubles as covered the face of the Earth when mankind started on its voyage.

Granted, then, that a static society must observe and enforce a rigid form of law, does it follow that, in comparison with a body of civilized men, it is any less active as measured by the intensity of its striving? It is not easy to provide a scientific answer to the question because we have not yet devised any accurate means of estimating the relative powers of the various human breeds. It is obvious that all that can be expected of a given brand of humanity is that it should live at the highest tension compatible with its innate capacity to balance output with organic wear and tear. Now it would hardly do, perhaps, to treat *Homo sapiens*, the specific type to which all existing branches of the human family alike belong, as a mutation established once for all in such a state of moving equilibrium that deviations from the average so far as they occur indicate no significant disturbance of the true-breeding quality of the race. At the same time the burden of disproof must, in the light of the known facts, rest on those who deny the approximate equality of the diverse ethnic stocks as regards intelligence and even physique, when acquired characters have as far as possible been written off, and regard is had solely to the norms exhibited by the congenital endowment. For our present purpose, then, we may postulate that the savage has it in him quite as much as the ordinary civilized man to reach a high standard of physical and mental exertion. What is more, one may go on to suggest that in practice he does attain this high standard of intensive living, although his method of doing so is not ours, but differs in a striking fashion which it may be worth our while to try to characterize a little more fully.

To cover the whole range of human history, we need two conceptions of progress—one as movement along a line, the other as movement in a circle. It would seem that either kind of energy is equally pleasing to mankind so long as the energy is in like degree unimpeded. If the former kind of progress can alone bring us nearer Heaven, the latter kind is presumably the only one available whenever we have got there. Now the primitive man envisages his earthly no less than his post-terrestrial paradise as an eternal round of the same activities raised to the nth point of smooth accomplishment. Whether in his native forest or in his happy hunting-ground he asks for no more than a beautiful continuance. Not for him do new machines advertise closer bondage under the specious guise of labour-saving comfort. Even new tunes, we are told, were not tolerated in the best days of ancient Egypt, though at this point Nature must have protested, to judge by the fact that the latest corroboree airs are wafted from end to end of aboriginal Australia. Yet it is no wonder that, having so little, the savage should stick fast to what he has got. He is like some poverty-stricken and lonely crofter who must hoard his mean substance and make it go as far as he can. Between him and starvation is nothing but his labour, his luck, and the little nest-egg represented by the capitalized experience handed on to him by his forefathers. In such narrow circumstances even a hovel-full of antiquated rubbish is not to be despised. For the sake of the odd clout or sherd that may serve for yet another turn of duty, the fusty reek of the rest is endured, and may even come to seem homelike; for the savage gets as much fresh air as he needs, or perhaps a bit too much for normal human lungs, on the weather-side of his dwelling. Present snugness rather than prospective fortune is all he asks of Providence; and, as in other cases, Providence sees fit to grant him what he seeks only if he prove sufficiently pertinacious and valiant in the seeking. Indeed, the main point that requires emphasis here is that both kinds of progress, the static and the dynamic, the roundabout and the point-to-point, entail equally hard work if they are to be achieved at all.

Now with savages such hard work falls hardest on the older men. We can speak, with Rivers, if we like, of 'gerontocracy', or greybeard government, by way of bringing out another aspect of the same fact; but there is at least as much onus as honour to be reckoned among the perquisites of such a stewardship. The task of a tribal elder is tiresomely manifold, because he presides over a social system which is Church, State, and University in one. The whole commonwealth conceived as a symbiosis composed of his ancestors, his contemporaries, and the rising generation is committed to his charge. Now it may well be that in a given case there prevails some doctrine of reincarnation to give symbolic expression to the implicit notion of life as a cyclical process; but even so the savage is too illogical, or too logical—it is a nice point which is the better way of putting it—to suppose that the spirit that returns to life has no need to start its schooling over again. Whether learning be rated with Plato and Wordsworth as a remembering or not, it proves in effect almost as tedious and unpleasant a business as being born; and hardly less

tedious and unpleasant is the job of the spiritual mid-
wife who helps to regulate the affair. Speaking as
one 'don' to another, I would congratulate the primitive gerontocrat on the general adequacy of his cur-
riculum regarded as an organ of educational mass-
production. Good, bad, or indifferent, his pupils
have to be levelled up to a standard of citizenship
which is not only absolute in theory, but in practice
varies so little that, barring interference from without, a secular duration can be predicted for any institution conducted soundly on stone-age lines. Now of
course nothing under the sun lasts for ever, not even
the hardiest specimen of these self-seeding growths
of the lower culture. Against our paltry seven thousand years of civilization must, however, be set the
probability that Tasmanians, Bushmen, or Eskimo
have, as Professor Sollas argues, been engaged for
perhaps twice that length of time in the more equable
occupation of pivoting on themselves like planets or
the seasons. Even if this be not strictly demonstrable,
one can be pretty sure that they were as little conscious of changing conditions to which they must
readapt their habits as we are, say, of those gradual
alterations of sea-level which by speeding up the geo-
logical cinematograph might easily be turned into a
nerve-shattering picture of the Deluge. The savage,
then, may be excused for behaving as if the larger
life of society were compromised in a *magnus annus*
—a revolving system with fixed and knowable orbit.
For the philosopher the theory may be true or it may

not. But for the primitive man it is valid, because he finds on repeated trial that it works.

Surely, then, from the standpoint of so totally different a world-plan, Stevenson's sneer at credulity can be seen to be misplaced if extended to experience and authority in their relation to the static type of society. Credulity must now be hailed as faith; and in an age of faith there can be no playing the fool with the things of the faith whether on the part of irresponsible youth or otherwise. The tribal elder feels himself as infallible as any pope; and the tradition of which he is the appointed minister and mouthpiece has for him all the force of a divine revelation. Knowledge he has at least in the pragmatic sense that it is knowledge of a well-tested way of life; and it seems to him an inspired knowledge inasmuch as ancestral precedent speaks not uncertainly therein. With Practical Wisdom, then, he is as conversant as was King Numa with the Nymph Egeria; but of her younger sister, the Speculative Intelligence, he has never encountered the rival attractions.

So much for primitive credulity on its intellectual side. But were it a mere faculty of knowing or opining, no amount of credulity, or, if we prefer to say so, faith, would move mountains. This is perfectly well known to the savage wonder-worker, to whom, by the way, the moving of mountains might well seem part of his ordinary routine, since staying the Sun, or bringing down the Moon, is clearly more of a feat as these things go. How, then, does one move moun-

tains, compel sun and moon, or what not? Any competent medicine-man would answer at once, 'By
mana'. So pregnant a word defeats all translation,
but it will perhaps suffice for the moment to say that
mana stands here for 'drive'. Only give him more
power to his elbow, and Man feels equal to shifting
the firmament, should it happen to be in his way.
But it would be unfair to judge humanity or human
religion by its partiality for miracles. Faith has its
journalistic department and miracles belong thereto,
being always news, and at their best propaganda.
Even to-day one may suspect that the public interest
in progress is rather skin-deep. Is it not true that
the novelties which science purveys from its labora-
tories—often, it must be confessed, with the air of
the artist who extracts a rabbit from a top-hat—appeal chiefly to an appetite for the marvellous which
has its roots far down in us and indeed is radical in
a racial sense? So too, then, in the static society they
must be tickled with novelties, though on the distinct
understanding that these are meant to enliven the
daily round but not to upset it. We need not, therefore, lay too much stress on the fact, if the elder in
charge of an initiation ceremony should indulge in
a few simple experiments in magic—*ad captandum
subsellia*—by way of diverting his class. How he
makes the boys stare every time that he brings up the
crystals from his inside! Now of course he is no
mere pedagogue, but a mystagogue in the most serious meaning of the term. These cheaper tricks, how-

ever, are but prolusory to the real mysteries. They are hardly more than exhibitions of professorial humour. As Godley, that Swan of Isis, sings *'Ad Lectionem Suam'*—'To his Lecture':

> I know thee well—nor can mistake
> The old accustomed pencil stroke
> Denoting where I mostly make
> A joke.

Now the practiser of these mild deceptions, even assuming him to be fully aware that they are such, is far too naïve to have excogitated any casuistical theory to the effect that the end justifies the means. At the same time if we, who stand at such a distance away that we can see the wood with the trees in due subordination to it, ask ourselves whether the initiation rites in their entirety are so contrived as to generate the necessary *mana* for maintaining the static society in being, there can be no doubt about the answer. The thing works; and herein lies the real miracle, such as puts all lesser ones into the shade. The upshot of these considerations is that credulity must rank as faith, a saving virtue so long as it supplies society with the drive required to keep it going, whether this be a going forward or simply a going round and round. For it must be remembered that a third possibility consists in going backward, and that in this direction the nature of the limiting condition, death, is clear, whereas in the other direction the goal, namely life, may be construed either as life positive or life superlative; so that mankind hardly knows whether to stand by its gains or to risk them on the chance of a 'maximum'. Now gambling may be excused in the rich, but the savage is a poor man whose chief solicitude is to keep the wolf from the door— in other words not to succumb to utter extinction, a monster not easily repelled by stone-age weapons. It is a perpetual puzzle to our Colonial administrators how easily a savage people collapses under treatment. Left to themselves these simple folk had fought the good fight for ages; yet, as soon as they come into contact with superior persons full of good intentions, their nerve seems to go, and it is too late to succour them. Fortunately it is beginning to dawn on the representatives of civilization that an imported faith cannot be substituted for a home-grown credulity except by means of a slow and delicate process of psychological grafting. Such a technique can be mastered only by the help of an anthropology which applies to each primitive society what is known as the 'functional' method of studying their indigenous culture. Borrowing a word from General Smuts, one might likewise describe this method as 'holistic'. Its object is to study the details of an organization in sole, or at any rate in primary, reference to their bearing on the effectiveness of the whole as a running concern. Thus it is opposed on the one hand to a method of origins which traces the back-history of the various factors, and on the other hand to a method of abstract valuation which considers how any one of these factors, taken individually, might be used

under different conditions in another and perhaps a
better way. Here, for instance, is a ship's stoker. As
regards origin, he may be a runaway solicitor or
merely a runaway schoolboy. Again, in point of abstract worth he may have in him the makings of a
peer or a pickpocket. But from the standpoint of the
captain of the ship, who is strictly functional and
holistic in his outlook, the immediate question is,
'Can the fellow stoke?' Functionally, then, the thirty-
nine articles of any savage faith hold true for those
concerned if they can likewise truly affirm that
crowning fortieth article: One and all together these
beliefs of ours enable us to live well here and now.

The instructiveness of a functional interpretation
of primitive religion is brought out with great clar-
ity in a short essay by Dr. Malinowski, who was indeed the first to give the method this descriptive
name, though anthropologists have long been acquainted with it *non verbo sed re*. His subject being
'Myth in Primitive Psychology', he exposes the in-
adequacy of the view which treats myth as typically
aetiological or explanatory in its aim, as if the savage were a philosopher who has nothing to do but to
scratch his head and ask 'Why?' of the universe at
large. But in stone-age society even the scratching of
one's head takes on a strictly functional significance.
Truth in the abstract has not yet come to be counted
among Man's daily needs. Thus, if one is expected to
swop one coin of scholarly mintage for another, myth
as assessed by its real function might be termed not

aetiological but fidejussive. Its business is not to satisfy curiosity but to confirm the faith. It is there to
cater, not for the speculative man with his 'Why?' but
for the practical man with his 'How if not thus?' As
Goethe says, *'Im Anfang war der Tat.'* 'Act first
and reflect afterwards' is good policy for cave-men in
their dealings with cave-bears. The environment of
the simple life is, so to speak, jumpy. Even so, Nature mercifully tempers the strain of coping with
constant emergency by consigning all secondary activities as far as possible to the charge of habit. Now
Habit is no sleeping partner in the business, since the
office-work must be kept up to the mark, if the head
of the firm, Attention, is to be left free to concentrate
on questions of make-or-break. On the other hand,
though highly competent within his own more limited sphere, Habit is prim and fussy, a martyr to
routine; wherefore it is only common sense on the
part of Attention to humour so useful a co-worker in
his little ways, however absurd. 'Be soople, Davie,
in things immaterial,' says the Rev. Mr. Campbell
to the hero of *Kidnapped*. To the same effect whispers the voice of Practical Wisdom in the ear of the
hard-pressed leaders of a primitive community.
Having their native share of shrewdness, they must
have their doubts about many a point of current belief. Indeed, it is possible, as I myself have done, to
accumulate an impressive heap of witness in respect
to the alleged scepticism of certain savage chiefs and
elders who, under cross-examination by the civilized

inquirer, have cheerfully allowed that augurs may
have cause to wink at one another in their private
capacity. Even if we suppose, as is quite likely, that
such confessions often form part of a general con-
spiracy to fool the white man, yet the very fact that
the native mind can distinguish between different
versions of the faith, whether the esoteric one be imparted to strangers or reserved for the initiated,
proves that one dead-level of credulity by no means
represents the psychological truth of the matter. I
venture, then, to suggest that, by proceeding on functional lines, one might, in any given case about which
the facts are sufficiently known, construct a scale of
religious values indicating how the primitive society
is aware of considerable disparity alike in the quantity and the quality of the *mana* attaching to different
ritual practices and notions. All that counts as medicine does not amount to 'big medicine' by a long way.
Though no savage would dream of applying the test
of credibility as such to the objects of his religious
appreciation, yet in his pragmatic way he can draw
some sort of line between that which is supereroga-
tory and that which is necessary and due. It may be a
little hard when very primitive folk are under investigation to distinguish these shades of significance, if
only because civilized sentiment finds it hard to do
justice to the inward appeal of endo-cannibalism,
blood-letting, phallic worship, and so on. If, however, a community of middle grade, as for instance
Ashanti, is examined from this point of view, it be-

comes clear in the light of what a sympathetic onlooker such as Captain Rattray is able to gather that
the natives are far from putting their High God,
their ancestral spirits, and the ignoble crowd of
fetishes, fairies, and hobgoblins on one and the same
plane of sanctity. On the contrary, a study of their
diversified pantheon proves that it implies gradations of rank which are almost equivalent to degrees
of reality so far as cult provides the criterion of religious truth.

Thus we are faced with an apparent contradiction.
On the one hand, the static society turns out to be not
incapable of discrimination between the greater and
the lesser things of the Law. On the other hand, it
represses all 'newness of spirit' and serves the law 'in
the oldness of the letter'—in a word, indiscriminately.
Why, then, we may well ask, does it thus prefer, in
Stevenson's words, 'to swallow the universe like a
pill?' Surely the answer is that the patient is thinking, not about his palate, but about his health. Let
the Speculative Intelligence suck the universe like a
sweet. The savage at the bidding of Practical Wisdom gulps down his bolus with such perverted gusto
that, the nastier it tastes, the more certain he is about
the virtue of his specific. Our custom, our whole
custom, and nothing but our custom—thus runs the
prescription. So in curative magic it is always the
rule that not a word must be varied if the formula is
to work.

Indeed, the same medical metaphor may be given

a deeper application. The very ideal of the static society, its subconscious standard of well-being, may be likened to health. Now, biologically speaking, namely, in reference to life which is a movement, health is the nearest thing to an absolute that is revealed immanently within human experience. The healthy man asks no more of his body than to keep healthy; for in relation to normal more could only mean too much, which is as bad as too little. In regard to health, then, the only sound policy is to let well alone. Though in reality life, however well-poised, is but an eddy in a perpetual drift, yet there is a passing sense of stability in revolving about a point. Thus faith is a sort of contentment with present fitness. Savages, we are apt to forget, enjoy being savage. They are not anxious to change places with us any more than we with them. The ptarmigan has no longing for the plain, nor the stormy petrel for enclosed waters. Science terms it adaptation to environment, but considered as a spiritual state it means possessing one's soul in peace, which in turn is an affair of feeling and keeping fit amid whatever circumstances one's lot may be cast. It is more a question of stoutness of heart than of the state of the weather; and indeed it may be formulated as a law that, climatically, the optimum conditions of human efficiency are more severe than those of human comfort. With the hard-pressed savage, then, the will to believe is equivalent to the will to affirm that life is never too hard so long as it is healthy. If his forefathers managed, he can manage also; and his chief concern is how the younger generation is to be taught to manage likewise. For, just as childbirth is always a critical period demanding medical attention, so the whole obstetrical art of assisting a soul into being by means of education implies that the social health is specially delicate in the matter of the reproductive function. If each year of freshmen is equal to the last, the institution may be trusted to carry on; but not otherwise.

To sum up, then, it would appear that the religious faith of the savage is not merely a will to believe a lot of nonsense. Nor, again, is it simply a will to take his world as he finds it, because in order to live up to such a hard world a man has to be fit, and fitness depends on *mana*. Now *mana* stands at once for miracle and for *morale;* and who will say that the savage is not right in identifying the two. With wonder and positive awe he discovers, as we all may do, that the moral order is capable of supplying out of itself the motive—the 'drive'—necessary to evoke moral action on the part of Man. This revelation comes, however, to the primitive man in a special way. So concrete-minded is he that he is bound to be more or less of a pantheist. He encounters the divine stimulus here, there, and anywhere within the contents of an experience in which percepts play a far more important part than concepts. The civilized man, on the other hand, thanks to a far wider system of communications which entails a free use

of mental symbols, favours a more abstract notion
of deity, seeking to grasp it in the unity of its idea
rather than in the plurality of its manifestations.
Now in both these directions there lies danger, but
in a different form. As for the savage, it is not a
starved intellectualism that he has to fear, but on the
contrary a sensualism nourished on a miscellaneous
diet that is mixed up with a good deal of dirt. Yet,
even though none of us may have reason to envy the
child of nature either for his innocence, or for his
digestion, the fact remains that he is uncritical of
his rough fare and can extract from it all the rude
health that a man can want. Whatever, then, may
be the final judgement of Ethics, a comparative history of Morals is bound to assume that among the
mixed ingredients of his religion the holiness prevails
over the uncleanness, since the vital effect is to
encourage him in a way of life that has survival
value. Thus, anthropologically viewed at all events,
the faith of the savage is to be reckoned to him for
righteousness.

VII

CONSCIENCE

Together with a blind allegiance to social convention goes sorrow at being out of touch with the rest and a desire to be restored to the fold. Though some sins are irremediable, others admit of rites of penance which remove the pollution, sometimes as if it were a physical foulness, but also, as in the rite of confession, by identifying it with a state of the mind; while the publicity of the humiliation helps to cast down the sinner in his own eyes. At the same time, a forgiveness which goes beyond strict justice is apt to inspire the penitent to repay the debt with interest.

A DELICATE problem of animal psychology is to determine the state of mind of the dog who, having purloined a delectable chop from the larder, has been duly discovered and arrested *adhuc flagranti crimine.* All the outward signs of a sense of guilt are present. His mien is doleful, his tail depressed. Yet, as regards his inward response to the distressing situation, which of the two are we to infer—sorrow for a commandment broken, or the fear of a prospective licking? Every lover of animals will know that the answer depends to some extent on whether the particular dog has a good master. If accustomed to sympathetic treatment, so that it has become a pleasure to act under the direction of the superior will, then a mere sense of being out of favour will suffice to induce a sort of penitential behaviour in a high-bred sensitive creature that perhaps has never actually felt the whip. Nay, even the most ravenous husky in a dog-team on the Yukon, though having a full and so-to-speak professional experience of the lash, will steal shamelessly from the tenderfoot who mishandles him, and yet will submit to rationing at the hands of a past master of the trail, repaying the harsh justice of his rule with a faithfulness that can curb, if it may never wholly dominate, the propensities of a wolfish nature.

Now a man is no dog. Though he may boast of belonging to the Wolf totem, the savage belongs to a higher order than that of the *Canidae*. We are therefore justified in attributing to his mental reactions a greater complexity than is displayed by those of any four-footed sinner that might make a show of repentance. In short, whatever we like to suppose about the animal, we have to credit the human being as such with the rudiments of a conscience. Now this term, though of familiar use in a religious or moral context, is on the whole avoided by the psychologist, no doubt because of a certain ambiguity in its current meaning. Thus what might be called a high-grade conscience, such as we can expect to find in the noblest type of civilized man, is hardly to be distinguished from the moral sense, which in its turn is much the same as the intuitional form of the moral reason. Thus at this level of intelligence conscience amounts to the *mens sibi conscia recti,* an apprehension of ethical principle or law in its universal character, that is, as applicable to all possible situations of the kind. On the other hand, it is only in a slight degree, if at all, that the savage appreciates right in and for its intrinsic reasonableness. Stevenson writes of one of his characters: 'his affections, like ivy, were the growth of time; they implied no aptness in the object'. Much the same might be said of the primitive man's respect for his ancestral custom; for what holds the social structure together is not the choice quality of the materials, but rather the fact that his heart-strings are entwined about it. His is therefore a sort of protopathic conscience capable only of a whole-or-none reaction to the stimulus of the familiar. It is a spirit of blind allegiance that cries, not 'My country, right or wrong!'—for that is to suppress a doubt—but 'My country for ever!', as if the course of plain but strictly local duty could not alter though the heavens should fall. The only conscientious objector known to savagery is the man in the next tribe, and he objects to everything. The home-bred offender against the decencies has not thought for himself, but on the contrary has simply forgotten himself. He is as a sheep that has gone astray, and can find no contentment until it rejoins the rest.

Such then, being posited as the general nature of the primitive or low-grade type of conscience, let us try to verify this conception of it by studying it more especially in its negative aspect, namely, as a conviction of sin. By so doing we may find it necessary to qualify Clifford's well-known definition of the savage variety of conscience as 'self-judgement in the name of the tribe'. As an attempt to do justice to its intellectual side this account may be all very well; for there is undoubtedly an exteriorization of the point of view, as if the tribesman could only think of himself in the third person and see himself as just one figure in the crowd. But there is also an emotional attitude to be reckoned with. So regarded, savage penitence would seem to amount to a home-sickness—the feeling of being lost conjoined with the desire to get back into touch. It may be worth while, then, to see how far such an interpretation will fit the evidence concerning the rules and measures of penance in the uncivilized society.

Let us start from the well-established psychological fact that sorrow, like fear, is a kind of 'asthenic' emotion, having as its direct and as it were reflex effect a tendency to depress the vitality for the time being—in other words, to subdue the spirits and to paralyse action. Whereas the healthy man, at peace with himself and with the rest of the world, enjoys being fit and does his best to keep so, a morbid state of nervous prostration is wont to induce a disregard and abandonment of self, so that for the utter weakling that way lies complete demoralization and perhaps suicide. Strangely enough, however, the opposite condition of blissful exaltation provokes similar transports of recklessness, as if to cast out care could only mean that anxiety and heedfulness must be banished together. Thus these two emotional extremes have at least this much in common that they give rise to what is to all outward appearance very much the same behaviour. 'I have heard', writes Thoreau, 'of Brahmins sitting exposed to four fires and looking in the face of the sun; or hanging suspended, with their heads downward, over flames; or looking at the heavens over their shoulders "until it becomes impossible for them to resume their natural position, while from the twist of the neck nothing but liquids can pass into the stomach". Or dwelling, chained for life, at the foot of a tree; or measuring with their bodies, like caterpillars, the breadth of vast empires; or standing on one leg on the tops of pillars.' These extravagances he sets down as 'forms of conscious penance', and it may well be that some such intention, whether fully explicit or not, is at the back of most of them, at any rate at the outset. But the Hindu ascetic would certainly claim that by thus tearing down the walls of the flesh he passes out into a rapturous freedom of the spirit. So, too, I have myself witnessed in the Sahara more than one of those exhibitions of self-torture in the course of which a frenzied fakir whirls about, cutting himself, chewing glass, and otherwise tormenting himself to the verge of utter physical break-down. The tourist may deem it a hoax or at most an affair of 'devil dancing', but to the native it is genuinely a 'God-seeking', the transcendent effort of an especially tough and valiant pilgrim to surmount the hardships of the true way. Science speaks airily about the 'masochism' of persons of the type of our European Flagellants; but no such sweeping phrase will serve to do justice to the endless gradations of emotional tone between the two poles of sorrow and gladness which occur within the religious consciousness when it probes its own wounds, whether self-inflicted or not, and makes a virtue and even a glory of mastering the pain.

Here, however, we are concerned primarily with the sorrowful side of this pivoting process, though it is undoubtedly its association with an incipient swing of the pendulum towards the joy of being restored to grace that distinguishes penitence from mere remorse, and gives it its value as a means of amendment. From a practical point of view remorse, being wholly retrospective, is a waste of time; whereas penitence is not only a prospective, but projective, seeking somehow to make good an anticipated forgiveness. Conscience in its most negative form is not like the daemon of Socrates which, according to the *Apology,* would from time to time hold him back, but never urged him forward. Rather it is a judgement of self-condemnation functioning as the active ally of the will to reform. It may indeed be that, so conceived, it lends itself to psychological definition less aptly than if it were taken simply as some principle of abstract thought. For morals, however, and more particularly for religion which has in view the spiritual welfare of the whole man, conscience can mean nothing less than a kind of motive, or moving reason, implying not only wisdom but guidance—words which, after all, come from the same root. Such a dynamic category is bound to part with most of its significance under the dissecting knife of an analytic psychology; whereas, if observed in its historical manifestations and according to the functional method, it can be plainly recognized for what it truly is, namely, an instrument of conversion.

First, then, what is the connexion between sorrow and sin? The question might seem superfluous to the moralist who disregards historical experience. Yet the anthropologist, when he bethinks himself of the eccentricities of any primitive system of taboos, may at first wonder how any one who, like Andrew Lang's 'Why-why, the First Radical', takes the liberty to infringe them should find himself one penny—or, let us say, one cowrie—the worse. Half these savage bogeys do not bite, or at any rate do not bite us. We are therefore disposed to distinguish between real and merely ritual offences, as if the latter had no binding force if considered in themselves and apart from some accidental convention. The objection to such a view of the matter is, of course, that no one actually concerned with these observances would dream of valuing them away from their immediate context. No doubt the ingenuous savage, more especially if helped on his way by a leading question, will improvise an explanation, probably on the lines

of so-called sympathetic magic, such as that if you
crack a marrow-bone you will interfere with the
resurrection of a sound animal, or perhaps will break
your own leg. But in all cases the real sanction is
that sacred custom forbids, that the thing is simply
'not done'. The law is the law, down to the least of
its injunctions. It is the holistic or wholesale conception of the moral code, such as always prevails in
the static type of society.

Hence, when Jevons finds in taboo an early form
of the Categorical Imperative, he is not far off the
truth, if this be taken simply to mean that particular
prohibitions exert an absolute claim to obedience on
the part of the primitive conscience. Another way
of putting the same thing is to call attention to the
automatic character of the supposed consequences of
their violation. Indeed, it is on the surface so like a
simple case of cause and effect that some anthropologists are chary of classing the infraction of taboo as
an offence against religion. Instead they propound
the ridiculously inadequate view that its import for
the savage is wholly magical, in the sense that it is
his apology for science, his would-be explanation of
a purely natural event. But for him there is almost
literally a world of difference between the sacred
and the profane; and because many a taboo is incidental to the common round it does not necessarily
descend to the level of the secular any more than
need be the case, say, with the institution of daily
prayers. Apart from the mechanization which all

social discipline as such is liable to import into human behaviour—and every established religion succeeds in imposing a drill—no ritual prescription can forfeit its right to rank among recognized dealings with unseen, wonder-working powers such as in their friendly aspect may be termed divine. Thus, taken in its connexion with the rest, the barest order to abstain from this action or that justifies itself as part of some supernatural design; and of this the end is fairly plain, though the means may be altogether obscure. For a primitive society has no use for casuistry. Had it reached the stage of picking and choosing among its moral conventions, it could proceed to resolve its separate cases of conscience by experiment, so that the event might enable the social reformer to be differentiated from the sinner. But the savage stands by his custom as a whole, in obedience to a pretty clear notion that it enables him to live; and, after all, he lives not because he obeys an order to that effect, but because he enjoys living. Moreover, this custom of his, which is his moral universe, is no machine that acts automatically, but rather a Providence; though no doubt it is a Providence which is expected to justify itself by its words. Whether we admire him for it or not, primitive man does not show much disposition to submit to an overruling destiny if it manifest itself simply in a neutral capacity. Thoroughly as he believes in the devil, he is not prepared to serve him. Nay, though surrounded with seemingly implacable forces, he imposes on the unknown his own moral demands and extorts an exhibition of worthiness as the price of his worship. Circumscribed and purely tribal in his outlook, he expects no sympathy from supernatural agencies alien to his social circle; while even within it there are to be dreaded the sinister influences which black magic is reputed to set in motion. Nevertheless, there is always a heart to his system of beliefs consisting in a supreme confidence in his tribal luck and in the sacred powers therewith concerned. His is not a diffused but a localized Providence, with a favour restricted to a single communion which, in the phrase of Robertson Smith, is 'theanthropic'—an association of the human with the divine. To belong to the chosen people is to enjoy the privilege of participating in their customary rites; for these constitute the ark of their strength, the very framework and foundation of the mercy-seat itself.

Meanwhile, the great difficulty encountered by the student who works backwards to primitive religion from the starting-point of an advanced theology is to make due allowance for the vagueness with which the savage conceives the agencies that thus control his tribal fortune. His one axiom is that they are good. Concerning their private nature, however, whether they are personal and in what degree, and so on, he imagines nothing very clearly; nor—what is more puzzling for us—does he demand any consistency from the play of his fancy. On the other hand, being perfectly definite in his mind about how to approach them in a ceremonial way, he lets them take their colour, as it were, from the ritual background of the moment. Sometimes they appear to answer to a mechanical mode of treatment, and sometimes to the way in which one man addresses another. In any case, the main business from the practical point of view is to reach and exploit the goodness which is always there. Now the only limitation to this goodness is a sort of latency out of which it has to be evoked into action. Convinced as to the fundamental benevolence, savage religion has likewise little doubt about the accompanying omnipotence, could it be energized to the full. To 'wait patiently for the Lord' may be beyond the scope of a primitive creed; but to cry 'Arise, O Lord' is almost as natural an impulse in the human being as it is for him to rebuke his own spirit and bid it take fresh courage. Thus a key to the way in which the divine power is held to be removed is provided by the way in which a man is moved or moves himself. Instead of studying the soul of the repentant savage in its blurred reflection, namely, a theology in which one might look in vain for any adequate idea of a God of mercy, one must fall back on a direct method of observing how the appropriate rites help him to acquire the dynamism that can bring about a change of heart.

How, then, does the primitive sinner envisage the sin which he acknowledges and would abolish by ritual means? Bearing in mind that exteriorization to which all his thoughts about himself are subject, we may expect him to see himself as marked off from the rest by some objectionable and clinging foulness. To break a taboo is to contract an infectious disease —a leprosy; and the leper must be banned as a danger to the herd. At first sight, however, to judge by the resulting loss of social rights, the man who wilfully breaks a taboo would seem to be in hardly worse case than he who is involved in one through no fault of his own. Having alike incurred pollution, both must undergo the same isolation, on preventive grounds that take no account of motive. Any man-slayer, for instance, is a public danger as being liable to be haunted, and that whether he has slain for good reason or for bad. Nay, those who mourn the death that he has wrongfully or rightfully caused find themselves in much the same plight, since the ghost —or to put it in a non-animistic way, the contagion of death—will assuredly dog their footsteps too. Friend or foe, just or unjust, they must sit together in outer darkness until the common miasma that is upon them lifts. Or again, it does not avail a woman that she is in no way responsible for various events inci-dental to her duties as a mother of the race; but she must be charged with an uncleanness which in itself counts almost for a shame, even if it implies a sacred-ness such as may redound to her glory in other phases of her life. Not to multiply examples, it can easily be shown that it is the crux of primitive ethics how to bring its awards of praise and blame into relation with the voluntary element in conduct.

Indeed, so long as the moral judgement has regard to outward forms only, there can be no chance of dividing the sheep from the goats—the ceremonially from the morally impure—seeing that externally there is blemish in them all. There may be a certain logic in making the innocent suffer with the guilty according to the principle of collective responsibility, as in blood-revenge; for kinship at a certain level of society is frankly recognized as a partnership for weal or woe. But it is an outrage on common sense that the confused notion of the sacred should provide a common denomination for the holy recluse and the accursed criminal. As it is, however, where thought thus conspicuously fails, practice alone could mitigate an impossible situation by assigning different terms to the allotted period of excommunication. Thus, whereas it might be well understood all along that the good man would in due season emerge from his enforced retirement to an intact position in society, the bad man could be condemned to outlawry or an indefinite sentence and perhaps for life. Now something of this sort undoubtedly happens in primitive jurisprudence, and an examination of the penal consequences of homicide would disclose the fact that a large discretion is actually exercised in exacting retribution, even when the strictest requital of 'an eye for an eye' is laid down by the prevailing code of law and honour. There is, in fact, an extreme degree of impurity which, juridically speaking at all events, lies beyond the reach of any plenary indulgence.

'Unhouseled, disappointed, unaneled', the doer of an unforgivable wrong either dies the death or, if allowed to escape, is cut off beyond hope of redemption.

On the other hand, it might be plausibly argued that this very insensibility of the savage to motive as the only ground of moral responsibility makes it easier for him to forgive and forget. For he is bound unconsciously to assimilate the unclean to the holy kind of sacredness, thus confounding a discreditable exile with a more or less meritorious withdrawal from worldly affairs. Thus the gracelessness of the former condition may take shelter under a quasi-positive valuation of taboo as a means of grace. Outwardly, at any rate, the one state can be changed and brought to an end as readily as the other. Because the savage wears his heart on his sleeve, a mere change of garment is enough to signify that he has put away his abominations and put on righteousness. As a piece of ritual mechanism, all that is needed is to substitute the linen for the sackcloth, and the thing is done. It is obvious, however, that such a symbolism is capable of more meanings than one, and that, as moral insight becomes clearer, it may be possible to read into it sentiments far more amenable to rational direction than the crude feelings that originally prompted the ceremonial act. Thus it would be interesting to inquire in detail how far the analogy of the mourner may not have helped to suggest that a befitting show of regret on the part of the sinner must precede any washing of his clothes and character. If Sir James Frazer is right in supposing that the wearing of mourning began as a disguise intended to deceive and so foil death with its attendant horrors, its significance as a sign of grief would be a secondary interpretation, a backstroke of the rationalizing intelligence. Of this, however, it could be proved that the humblest savages are capable, as, for instance, the Arunta widow who explained her apparel of white paint—white over black being equivalent to black over white—as meant to exhibit to her husband's spirit the sincerity of her sorrow. Similarly, then, if purification has thus come to be associated with a deliverance from grief, the criminal admitted to purgation might get the benefit of a transferred compassion from those who beheld his trappings of woe; while, again, in his own person he would learn to regard his own lamentable condition as a reason why he should himself lament instead of hardening his heart from turning.

Nevertheless, despite these possibilities of reinterpretation, a ritual which consists in the removal of a foulness of the outer man, such as dust and ashes, or the stain of blood, or defiled garments, is not suited to express the travail that must accompany the workings of conscience, because as a means of grace it seems altogether too easy—a mere affair of ridding the surface of an offensive incrustation. It is true that some savages, though by no means all, take no pleas-

ure in washing themselves in the ordinary way; nor
is the sweat-bath in its primitive form an entirely
agreeable way of subjecting the body to strong and
remedial medicine. Also there are uncomfortable
scarifications and singeings that may qualify the tender mercies of a savage lustration. Yet for the most
part the stress is laid on the efficacy of the detergent
process rather than on the spiritual effort required
of the subject. The Aleut, too near the Arctic to be
a lover of cleanliness, places grass against his person
that it may absorb his sins, and then consigns the
grass to the fire. The Ancient Peruvians during a
purificatory ceremony would stand at their doors
shaking imaginary dust from their clothes that it
might be blown away into the surrounding air. Or,
again, all over the world it is a well-known device to
bathe in running water that the evil may be carried
off and out to sea. Thus, in general, one may perhaps
say that among savages the use of holy water is want-
ing in inward reference, no doubt because they are
relatively sense-bound, and incapable of raising a
mechanical symbolism to the level of a spiritual
metaphor. It is not so hard for a simple mind to picture clean hands as a clean heart. True, the Mexican
priest in baptizing a child said not only 'may that
water wash away all that is evil' but also 'may it
whiten thy heart'. But after all he was half civilized
and correspondingly may be said to halt half-way
between an exterior and an inward-seeking view of

the virtue of his act. A cruder imagery is needed to convey to the savage that his sin has truly been expelled from within him.

Now in many a primitive psychology heart and stomach stand for very much the same thing, namely, as the seat of the affections, such as are by no means entirely carnal. Nay, what we call the mind may in turn be brought under the same inclusive category; and, after all, the observable effect on the mind of eating and drinking, indirect though the process may be, is not small. Now, as is well known, the savage is religiously particular about what he eats, so that his list of forbidden foods is apt to run to astonishing lengths. Moreover, he is well acquainted with fasting as a mode of humbling and chastening the soul. Naturally a gormandizer, as any one might be who was none too certain about the source or the quality of his next meal, he nevertheless can rigidly control his appetite in response to a ritual obligation, and learns to measure his spiritual welfare in terms of his power over the flesh. No wonder, then, that with him a strong heart becomes synonymous with an empty stomach. It follows that, in order to be void of offence, he must painfully scour his internal parts. Without going into unpleasant details, one may note that a catharsis in the physical sense is a common accompaniment of ceremonies of purification, such as notably those that precede a rite of renewal such as a feast of first fruits. Thus old Adair notes how certain American Indians of his day would before harvest, or, again, before starting on a campaign, purge themselves with button-snake root; and goes on to translate the native name for the custom as 'the expiation of sin'. Such a method of cleansing the inner man provides a method of throwing off impurity of all kinds; for we hear of medicine societies among the Pueblo Indians whose members, before a celebration of the mysteries, must undergo not only strict continence but an emetic each morning for four days in order to remove the taint of their previous conjugal relations. Materialistic, then, though the ritual remains in the form of its expression, it has got one step nearer to a representation of the inwardness of a true, that is, heartfelt, repentance.

The next step is from emptying the stomach to emptying the soul; and here we begin to come within sight of conscience as a mental function, even if to think of mind as a receptacle that can be emptied and filled involves us in spatial metaphor of a rather crude order. Meanwhile, to the Akikuyu who use one and the same word for the ritual use of an emetic and for the confession of sins that accompanies it there is probably no discernible difference between the two processes, since both alike relate to some central organ on which his health and happiness seem to depend. In Ancient Mexico the sinner confessed his iniquities, in the presence of a priest, to a goddess known as 'Eater of impurities'—as if the most irritating matter must yield to a divine digestion. Indeed, from native America comes the evidence of a widespread practice of confession not only as customary throughout the Andean civilizations but as also extending northwards to hunting tribes such as the Plains Indians, the Iroquois, and the still more backward Athapascans. Closely associated as this rite always is with acts suggestive of the removal of some filthy or disgusting substance, it must be set to its credit as a medium of religious self-education and self-discipline that it enables sins to be faced under their true names and thus to some extent in their true nature as it is for thought. Though in the mass they may be rated as a kind of impurity or dirt, yet if murder or adultery or even some purely ceremonial offence is confessed *eo nomine,* the moral consciousness can no longer be said to be working in the dark. No doubt words count more or less as things for the savage, and it is the very naming of his misdeeds that make it possible to get a purchase on them and lift them like a weight from off his chest. But words likewise afford fixed points on which feelings and ideas gradually form up in an increasingly coherent order. It may be that in religious experience precision of meaning is no final test of value; yet certain it is that religion enters on a new phase, marked by an intellectual grasp of principle unknown before, when a mechanical type of ritual, amounting to no more than a kind of gesture language, gives way to one in which oral forms have come to prevail. Moreover, as the other institutions of society, political, legal, economic, and so on, invariably pursue a similar course of development, religion could hardly refuse to follow suit, unless at the risk of losing its historic right to preside over all the practical disciplines and keep them true to a single and sublime purpose.

Meanwhile, in view of the many-sided nature of conscience, confession needs to be considered in relation not only to thought but also to the will. For to acknowledge one's fault in public is to conjoin self-knowledge with self-surrender, the harder thing of the two. For the savage especially, who beholds himself chiefly as others behold him, thus to humiliate himself in the sight of all is an experience almost more bitter than death; though on the other hand he is inclined for the same reason to give way to drama and, like the mourner, to make a gazing-stock of his very afflictions. In any case he stands up before all to take his medicine, so that his conscience may be void of offence. The criminal has given himself up and thrown himself on the mercy of the court. He is not as the rebel against society who in the stubbornness of an evil heart puts up a fight and, if overtaken, dies defiantly like some Red Indian warrior at the stake. Such is indeed, according to primitive morals, the proper attitude of a man in his relation to the rest of the world, his natural foes. But towards his own communion even the excommunicated man should feel, like Socrates in prison, that he has no right to violate his side of the contract. Whatever taboo he may have broken, and however much he may deserve

to be exorcized and expelled like an unclean spirit,
yet he is no stranger but an exile, with a home-sickness, and hence with at least a potential loyalty, ever
ready to stir the depths of his heart. No doubt, by
encouraging the culprit to confess, the court has of
its own accord hinted that its favour is not finally
withdrawn, but that on the contrary a contrite behaviour may earn a mitigation of the sentence. Even
so, a certain spontaneity is required of the prisoner
at the bar if he is to meet the concession in the spirit
in which it was made. He must make a clean breast
of it freely and even gratefully. He must be forward
to grasp the extended hand, must not merely accept
but seek the proffered pardon.

Justice, then, even divine justice, is conceived by
the savage as tempered with mercy towards the
offender who 'repents to the acknowledging of the
truth'. In saying so, however, let us not fail to make
due allowance for that scenic quality which a mind
working chiefly at the sensitive level imports into all
its proceedings, and more especially into those that
take place in public. In order to make a scene of it
the primitive actor invariably overplays the part; or
so at least it would strike the civilized observer, the
man in the stalls. Even in enlightened Athens emotional displays occurred such as no modern court
would tolerate; and to move the pity of the jurors
regular tragedies were staged with choruses of weep-
ing women and so forth. Now under stone-age conditions one may well suppose that the feelings are

even more under the sway of the excitement of the moment. This very fact, however, makes for a kind of forgiveness which is really more like a forgetting of injuries. The mind passes from one emotional context to another without noticing the transition, just as a crying child can be solaced with a toy. Thus when Australian black-fellows have thrown their spears and boomerangs to their hearts' content at the accused party, who dodges the missiles passively according to the custom known to anthropologists as that of the expiatory exposure, they let him off if still unscathed, no doubt mainly because they have worked off their wrath, and are ready for the next thing on the programme, as for instance a meal. This comes out very clearly in their alternative custom of allowing accuser and accused to batter each other on the head with clubs, with the sportsmanlike proviso that the accused shall have the first blow. When each has had enough, then in their own language their hearts have become 'cool'. Thus they hardly need to switch off a passion that has burnt itself out. So, then, any penitential rite among savages is apt to display a marked exhibitionism. Because of their groanings will it repent the divine powers. Some of these, indeed, are implacable, like the Furies, the avengers of kindred blood. But there may be remission of lesser sins, such as slaying outside the clan, a matter for which the law allows composition. Even so, however, a righteous indignation must be propitiated by crying loudly and abjectly for mercy. The Indian brave, who would never demean himself by whining to a human foe, yet howls 'O Wakanda, pity me!' in the extremity of his self-humiliation. Further, whereas the pains that he inflicts on his body may be a source of secret pride since they testify to his endurance, an open confession of his transgressions cannot but cut him to the heart, being utterly contradictory to that spirit of self-esteem which causes him to boast of his achievements and rejoice in any sort of public ovation. In short, his tribulation is not merely symbolic and affected, but real. He has descended to the depths, and from the depths comes his plea for pity. He may have no clear idea of the Being whom or which he is trying to move. Sometimes there is a clear implication of personality, as when an anthropomorphic deity or the body of tribal ancestors is being appeased; and sometimes it is as if an impersonal curse were being automatically lifted. In either case, however, before any alleviation of the situation becomes possible, the asthenic effects of a great sorrow must have been experienced to the utmost. The sinner must first be cast down in his own eyes no less than in the sight of all.

It remains to inquire how this weakness can be turned into a renewed strength. Looking at the question more especially from the side of the emotions, one can assume it to be true of any passion that, the further it retires, the further it is likely to leap. The excited man is like the fever-patient who swings across normal-point without knowing it and can only feel either too cold or too hot. Thus there is always a danger lest old sinner should imagine himself new saint without coming any nearer to that state of quiet and reasonable assurance which, like a steady pulse, is an index of moral health and balance. If religion is to further and consummate the work of conscience, it must so contrive that, having rescued his feet from the depths and turned his face towards the heights, it should recall the wayfarer to his immediate duty which is to climb as before. M. van Gennep in his brilliant book *Les Rites de Passage* has shown how many types of primitive ritual conform more or less to a triple movement in which, first, a severance from the world is represented, then a communion with the divine, and, lastly, a return to the world, though on a new and higher plane of it. Without attempting here to force the facts about primitive modes of penance into such a rigid framework one may note how, in helping a man to wipe out his past and regain his forfeited position in society, they likewise bring him, at the supreme moment of the oscillation from misery and shame to happiness and restored honour, into touch with a mystery, a miracle, *mana,* so that his life can never afterwards be quite the same. Whereas justice is a cold principle, implying a calculable correlation of rights with duties, there is a magic in forgiveness—an unreason which is a super-reason in that it works wonders. Here conscience finds its true dynamic, namely, in an

emotional tendency of the unstable character to give
itself the benefit of the doubt when met half-way by
a like spirit in others. Instead of reciprocity there
is offered an unmerited love, an unmeasured rejoic-
ing over a lost but very average sheep; and, by a
mystical contagion of warmth, a responsive generos-
ity is kindled in the recipient of the bounty. As the
phrase goes, he takes heart of grace. The prodigal
has been feasted on *mana* at the tribal expense; and,
as on the north-west coast of America one *potlatch*
calls for another—that is, an extravagant distribution
of goods must be matched by the receivers of pres-
ents with even more extravagant distributions in
return if they would not 'lose face'—so the freely
imparted *mana* is a debt of honour that must be paid
with interest. Whether the ardency of this resolve
to make good and even transcendently good can be
maintained on the return to the day's work remains
to be seen. But to have suffered is to learn. Conscience may be educated so as to bear a fuller witness.
Thus it may be that the pardoned deserter will be
found in the forefront of the next battle; for conscience can make heroic cowards of us all. For the
rest, religion with its organized ritual of penance,
pardon, and rehabilitation imposes on society as a
whole a view of life which tends to class all its evils
under the head of moral evil for which the other ills
are chastisements. It then pronounces moral evil to
be remediable by grace if not by merit—that is, by
experiencing and in turn willing the something more

that exalts love above interest, goodness infinite
above such goodness as men apportion to each other
by rule and measure.

It turns out, then, that the savage is not as the dog
who slinks away when in disgrace, or at most sub-
mits cringingly to the whip. Thanks to an altogether
higher endowment of will-power, the man consents
to his whipping and might almost be said sometimes
to whip himself. His various rites of atonement do
not merely reflect a futile self-pity. He makes a virtue of a painful necessity by learning to value endurance, humility, meekness for themselves as better
than the vainglory of one who cannot own himself
in the wrong. For a savage who in his fiercer moments prides himself on behaving like a wolf, it is no
small step towards self-mastery and self-direction to
have acquired tenderness of conscience even in this
degree. So touchy about his honour as he is, he lets
himself be shamed when he has sinned and the *mana*
is withdrawn from him, and knows that there is
nothing for him but to go through with it until he is
forgiven. Only when he is taken back to the bosom
of the tribe will his *mana* return. Then, the spell
upon him broken by a stronger medicine, the warrior
can go back to the fighting line.

VIII

CURIOSITY

In treating the pursuit of knowledge as a mystery for which a moral discipline must form a preparation primitive religion effectively refutes that shallow interpretation of its rites which, because an appeal to a god is not always in evidence, deems them self-sufficient and arrogant in their underlying spirit. On the contrary, the novice at initiation, the member of the secret society, the theocratic ruler, and the craftsman must one and all purchase their enlightenment at the cost of a rigorous training, while the door of the sanctuary remains closed to unqualified persons.

AT the root of those intellectual virtues which make up the truth-seeking and truth-enjoying part of human nature at its best lies a certain itch for knowing. This in itself, however, is no virtue, but an ambiguous tendency needing careful direction if it is to yield a benefit clear of all drawback. Thus the Latin word from which curiosity is derived is apt to carry with it an implication of excess. Nay, the rhetorician Quintilian who delights in distinguishing fine shades of meaning defines *curiositas* as *supervacua operositas*—the uncalled-for industry of a busybody; and goes on, somewhat cryptically, to declare that the difference between the diligent and the curious man is on a par with the difference between religion and superstition. It would seem, then, that in the opinion of the ancient world a line was to be drawn between religious zeal and a perversion of it which would doubtless include a perverse taste for prying into mysteries. On the other hand, the modern attitude towards the mysterious is somewhat harder to determine. Thus science may on the whole be said to regard the inexplicable as a monster to be slain after the manner of St. George; and it can actually claim to have administered the death-blow to many a hoary and foul chimaera. Philosophy, again, is inclined to recognize but one supreme mystery consisting in the allness or altogetherness of the universe. As for religion, it might be supposed that a certain mysticism constituted its very essence. It is doubtful, however, whether every contemporary theologian would yield a full assent to such a view, as, for instance, the author of the remark that mysticism begins in mist and ends in schism; and in any case one may be sure that, if accepted at all, the principle would be interpreted and applied in all sorts of conflicting ways.

Speaking generally, however, of the intellectual world of to-day, there can be no doubt that the prevailing tendency is to refuse to tolerate any unknowable, and to treat the merely unknown, not as something to be revered from a distance, but rather as something to be approached and overcome. Even if the robust optimism of the Victorian age is to-day a little out of fashion, our generation would still be prepared to declare with Robert Browning, 'Whatever there is to know, that we shall know some day.' Now of course this is essentially an aspiration on our part, even if some of us prefer to state it in the form of an axiom. We cannot both know and not know, at any rate in the same sense. Reckoning it, then, simply as an article of faith, we have at the same time to allow that, of all our present creeds, none is more firmly or widely embraced than this belief in the attainment of knowledge as an unconditional good in prospect.

But it has not always been so. Time was when heaven seemed to frown on the overbold inquirer. It amounted to wanton insolence for men to desire to be as gods knowing good and evil. How far, then, can we as students of human history explain this violent contrast of opinions? Not that it is possible on historical grounds to decide the question of value. We can, however, hope to obtain a better idea of the advantages and the risks attendant on the pursuit of truth by consulting the experience of the ages, formed as it has been under all sorts of changing conditions. Primitive man had plenty of cause to realize that 'a little learning is a dangerous thing'. After all, to blaze a trail through virgin country is a treacherous business as compared with comfortable travel in the wake of the surveyor and the engineer. Whether, then, it is for the Fall of Man or rather for the Ascent of Man that curiosity is to be held

responsible in the long run, we must for anthropological purposes take for granted its inherent ambivalence, its power to heal or to hurt. In other words,
we may expect to find evidence not only of the use,
but likewise of the abuse, of the inquisitive temper
as it has influenced the development of primitive
religion.

In a previous lecture it was argued that hope
rather than fear is the chief driving force behind all
human religion. Small wonder, then, if man, more
manipulative by natural endowment than any monkey, and hence inclined to paw everything that he
comes across, should imaginatively claim the entire
universe as his plaything. Even if he stings his fingers all too frequently as a consequence, he stead-
fastly refuses to take this as a hint to mind his own
business. In short, he conceives the human sphere
as ideally conterminous with the divine; for whatever baffles his natural powers in the first instance he
deems eventually subject to his mastery, thanks to
supernatural means that he hopes somehow to bring
within his reach. What presumption in a low-born,
if a decidedly high-brained, creature! Yet too large
a measure of humility in his emotional composition
might have left him for ever embogged in the
primeval slime of animal instinct. We may perhaps
console ourselves with the reflection that, if a certain
immodesty is a condition of emergence, the upstart
is wont to mend his manners when once he has made
good.

Now it is a commonplace of anthropology to contrast the religious man who has learnt to say 'Thy will be done' with the magician who says 'My will be done', and if signs and wonders happen to follow claims all the credit for them. Further, Sir James Frazer makes magic older than religion, and believes that it was only when the magician's pretentions had proved to be hollow that men at length bowed down before gods, that is, beings whom they had come to conceive as altogether superior in power to themselves. This indeed I regard as a rather questionable piece of history; for I do not believe that primitive man was so clear-headed or so critically disposed as to abandon magic because he judged it an imposture or simply a practical failure; more especially seeing that plenty of people who have enjoyed a civilized education are unable or unwilling to break with magic now. On the contrary, I suspect that there was no sensible breach of continuity between the more or less godless kind of wonder-working rite, which in point of time may well have been prior, and the kind in which the intermediation of gods is explicitly invoked; for which reason I would prefer to extend the term religion to cover both stages of what I take to have been one organic development. This change in the angle of vision, however, scarcely affects the question how far men originally confronted the unknown in a spirit of arrogance, which was only by degrees chastened into one of abasement as the conviction grew that to tempt Providence is to ask for trouble.

My own view about the matter is that any arrogance discoverable in the most primitive type of rite —which we may class as magico-religious, so as to leave the problem of magic *versus* religion out of account—is mostly on the surface. The real difference between this and the more developed method of dealing with the occult is that the former is dramatic rather than oral in its leading forms of expression. So long as a meaning is conveyed by dumb-show rather than by word of mouth, there is likely to be a certain air of self-sufficiency about the whole performance, as if what had to be done was done duly and in effect; whereas there is bound to be some suggestion of deferred action in a verbal formula, even if its tone be that of command rather than of petition. Externally viewed, then, the dramatic kind of rite might well seem to involve less chance of disappointment, and to a corresponding extent less need of some supplementary agency that would serve to help the action out. If, however, we try as best we can to enter into the feelings of those concerned, it becomes by no means so certain that their mood is dictatorial, or is even comparable to the quiet assurance of the man who is master of his trade. Thus the parallel which Sir James Frazer would draw between sympathetic magic (as he calls it) and the physical science of to-day seems to me to be on psychological grounds unsound. The savage, I believe, is perfectly aware of the difference between killing his enemy by striking him and killing him by striking at him through his image. That a man should die of a well-directed blow is a matter of course—something that happens in the ordinary course of events. But manslaughter by proxy is an outrage on common experience and common sense. It is monstrous that a display of sham-fighting should prove as deadly as real warfare. Nay, this is likewise how the victim feels about it. Though ready to stand up to a visible foe, he quails before such an attack in the dark. With Ajax he is fain to cry:

> If we must perish we thy will obey,
> But let us perish in the light of day!

In a word, the symbolic rite as such has to do with the uncanny. That it works is not questioned; but how it works passes the understanding of the plain man.

Does the expert see any further into the mystery? Does he, for instance, consider himself to be merely experimenting with principles borne out by daily use and wont, such as that like is apt to beget like, and the part to reproduce the whole? I venture to doubt whether he pursues any such line of thought even a little way. On the contrary, no one is more ready than he himself to believe that he is in touch with another world, having arbitrary ways of its own to which he is yet somehow privy by reason of his special craft. Such surely is the purport of his claim, whatever we may think of its validity. Nor should we confine our attention to that dubious type of trafficker with the occult who works more or less alone, namely, the sorcerer, or professor of magic, in that unfavourable sense of the word which is likewise, I think, the most appropriate. Let us study rather the case of one who takes a leading part in a mimetic rite of a communal and hence respectable kind, as for instance a totemic ceremony. Such a man is a mystagogue and he knows it. He is assisting at a miracle. The means taken and the end sought are to outward appearance unconformable. Hence, in the absence of any physical nexus capable of uniting them, a hidden link must be supplied from the side of the sacred; and the sacred is always the spiritual.

To put the same thing in a more concrete way, it is not profane but sacred lore that can alone yield assurance of success in any mystic operation; and sacred lore is knowledge pre-conditioned by a spiritual discipline. Of course the hierophant requires a technique; but this is not on a par with the technique of the ordinary craftsman, except in so far as the latter does his best to promote his craft to the status of a genuine mystery. Religious knowledge implies a religious education. The price of *mana* is taboo—a certain withdrawal into self and away from the outer world and its concerns. In Australia, for instance, no participation in sacred rites is possible except for the initiated, and initiation often has many grades which promise greater enlightenment in strict proportion to the increased severity of the preliminary preparation. That the flesh is duly mortified in the course of such an ascending process may be gathered from the fact that among the Arunta a hole bored through the tongue is the mark of a full doctorate. *Il faut souffrir pour être saint.* Nor does the body bear all the brunt of such a training, while the mind is neglected or at best allowed only to profit indirectly. There is evidence in plenty to show that instruction is freely imparted to the novice by oral means eked out with pantomime. Even the completed doctor does not set out to practise at once, but for about a year's space is wont to devote himself to meditation, so that the spiritual effects of all that he has been through may be completely assimilated. Nor even now has he done with his self-repressions—his taboos. Various abstinences accompany his entire career, and condition his efficiency so absolutely that, if ever his self-control breaks down—as when a certain medicine-man succumbed to European strong drink—he has the decency to retire from the profession. Because this man had proved unworthy, the inspiration had departed; sanctity would not cohabit with sin. His *mana* was gone, or in other words his assurance had left him.

Thus it is a shallow view that would impute to the primitive wonder-worker a brazen cocksureness derived chiefly from the ease with which he can impose upon his fellows. Rather in the typical instance— and the student of mankind must be prepared to contemplate our race at its best and not merely at its worst—his confidence is that of the athlete at the top of his training, who is poised but tense—all nerves, but with his nerves in control. The need of screwing himself to the required pitch of dynamic energy is all the greater because he will in all likelihood be one who is constitutionally liable to violent oscillations of feeling. For primitive society sees to it that the graduates in such a school come of carefully selected stock. After all, every youthful male is put through his paces at the ordinary initiation; so that any special aptitude for experiences of the mystic type is soon detected. Hence only those naturally qualified—the kind of folk, for instance, who can see ghosts—proceed by way of an intensified training to the higher degrees in divinity. Now it is easy to depreciate this type of mind, more especially as it occurs under conditions of savagery, by the free use of terms such as 'hysterical', 'dissociated', 'introverted', and so on; but it should at least be in fairness noted that such adjectives would equally well apply to the majority of civilized folk who show themselves unusually susceptible not only to religion but to the higher culture in any of its leading forms. There is at least a grain of truth in the French saying *tout savant est un peu cadavre*. To be a little dead to the passing impressions of the sense-world is the prime condition of possessing a soul of one's own.

Further, the exterior aid needed to promote such withdrawal into self is leisure, not to say solitude.

When we consider how savages are for the most part accustomed to huddle together like sheep, so that all privacy as we understand it is utterly impossible, it is somewhat amazing that in the mechanism of social institutions elaborate provision should be made for those in need of a time of spiritual retreat. We are not indeed to suppose that the meditations induced by such retirement into the wilderness are of the articulate order; being presumably rather in the nature of vague stirrings felt somewhere below the threshold of manifest consciousness. Even so, the net result is that, in a metaphor familiar to native Australia, a 'new birth' is experienced. There occurs a conversion into a more potent because a more self-knowing kind of man, who to satisfy his new-found needs is emboldened to call a new world into existence; which world is, however, in its essence not material but moral. So much, then, for the education of the will to know, as the ruder savagery provides it for the elect.

What, however, of those whom a jealous policy of guarding the mysteries keeps out in the cold? Let us admit that a principle may be sound, although particular applications of it are open to criticism. Thus on the one hand it is reasonable to hold that revelations are not for the unprepared, that knowledge worthy of the name is the fruit of a long and painful initiation. So far, then, the old-world ritual warning, *Procul o procul este, profani!* 'let the unsanctified keep their distance', is necessary and just. On the

other hand it is equally clear that enlightenment
should be made a matter of desert, not of privilege;
whereas it is unfortunately true that human society
has ever been remiss, as compared with Nature, in
discriminating between fit and unfit. No doubt Australia shows itself none too merciful towards the unworthy, as when the youth who behaves irreverently
during the course of the initiation rites is promptly
speared by the elders in charge. Here is examina-
torial purgation with a vengeance. Yet who in these
days would venture to endorse the aboriginal attitude
in regard to the higher education of women? If elsewhere the female sex is found to indulge in mysteries
of its own, and can retaliate by threatening male intruders with the fate of Pentheus, there is no hint of
any such equivalence of rights in this most backward
province of the human world. Here, evidently
labouring under the impression that 'Curiosity, thy
name is Woman', the men take the most drastic measures in order that their secrets may be shrouded from
feminine eyes. When a lady is required by custom to
cover her head with an opossum rug during the progress of a ceremony, her opportunities of observation
are curtailed. Even so an old *gin* has been known to
boast to a white man that she had managed to ferret
out far more about the tribal *arcana* than any member of her sex was supposed to know; though no
doubt it would have been suicide to confess as much
to her husband. Indeed, there can be little doubt
that it is the deliberate intention of the wiseacres who

control affairs to ensure what Mill would call the
'subjection' of women by keeping them ignorant and
in like measure superstitious. Thus the novices who
have just passed through the first stage of their initiation, so that henceforth they rank as men instead of
boys, are encouraged to celebrate their acquisition of
the manly virtues by engaging in a ceremony which
bears the straightforward name of 'frightening the
women'. The fun—not to say the moral obligation—
consists in whirling bull-roarers in the dark round
about the women's camp; and, whatever the poor
creatures may really think about it, they are at least
officially supposed to regard it as the authentic voice
of Hobgoblin, and by their consequent terrors to be
duly reduced to a state of passive obedience. It
should be observed, however, that this religious dis-
franchisement of a whole sex represents the only kind
of class-legislation that occurs at this low level of
society. For menfolk there is complete equality of
opportunity, and no modern democracy could offer
more in the way of an educational ladder, whereby
every born climber is bound to find his way to the
top.

At this point, did time allow, we ought to go on to
examine the age-long and world-wide history of
secret societies—a complex and obscure subject. This
constitutes the first or, if we treat tribal initiations
under a distinct head, the second chapter of the history of human education. Indeed, any member of an
American university, I imagine, has a better chance

of realizing this connexion between education and secret rites than one who like myself bears neither upon his mind nor on his person the sacred brand of the catechumen. Or, again, it is well known to the classical scholar that Plato's *Republic,* which still holds its own as the world's foremost treatise on education, draws freely on the mysteries of ancient Greece not only for its imagery but even for its leading idea, namely, that all advance in true knowledge is a conversion, a Pilgrim's Progress from darkness towards the light, a *catharsis* aiming at the liberation of the spirit through the mortification of the flesh. Historically, then, there is strict continuity between the clear-sighted ideals of those who direct and actually pursue the higher studies of to-day and the dim and groping sentiments that prompted primitive religion to shield the narrow path to truth and reality from the intrusion of unqualified persons. It is against reason and instinct alike that the Sacred Way should be open to profane traffic.

Now the origins to which secret societies may be referred are diverse, the term being loosely used to cover institutions of very various types which agree only in a stubborn unwillingness to make their proceedings public. Initiation ceremonies, however, almost certainly rank among the more important of the contributory influences; and, since the sexes are always initiated apart, one may conjecture that they are especially connected with associations that maintain a rigid sex-exclusiveness as contrasted with those

which, as happens quite frequently, seek their re-
cruits indifferently among men and women. Indeed,
whereas at the most primitive levels of tribal life sex
together with age provides the only ground of social
differentiation, clanship otherwise conferring equal
rights on all, a new criterion of status has come into
force by the time that the secret society emerges into
prominence. This is the principle of aristocracy.
Such a change may be caused from within or from
without. It may be due to the growth of wealth and
the rise of powerful clans or families at the expense
of the rest; while in other cases conquest or even
peaceful penetration on the part of a higher culture
is able to bring it about. Such a governing class, whatever the source of its power, must maintain it by impressing the imagination of the rest. Kingship, nay,
the modern state itself, has evolved out of the inco-
herent mobbishness of mere tribalism by the sheer
force of a doctrine of divine right. Thus a primitive
aristocracy is always a theocracy. Statecraft and
priestcraft reinforce each other, and both together
owe their imputed majesty to a calculated remote-
ness. Esotericism, in a word, is the invariable accompaniment and condition of the centralization of authority. Even under a clan-system the dominance of
the male over the female or of the old man over the
young is secured in this way. Later on there arises
a class-system when, as Herbert Spencer would say,
not only a nucleus but a nucleolus, a still more concentrated principle of directive energy, has been

separated out of the social tissue; whereupon the extent of the gap between lowest and highest, between the most passive and the most active elements in the body politic, is correspondingly increased. As heaven is divided from earth, so is the divine king from his people. Nor must it be thought that such royalty entails no obligation to live up to the part. The vice-regent of the gods is subject to those laws that demand physical and moral fitness in the initiated man, nay, must make and keep himself supremely fit inasmuch as his grade of initiation is the highest of all. Such a book as *The Golden Bough* is full of information about the austerities incumbent on the person or body of persons in charge of the primitive state, in which sanctity and sovereignty go strictly together. One hears less, however, about the intellectual side of the ruler's life. Yet it would be easy to cite examples of hard-working students of high degree. They range from the Maori chief, who must have unfalteringly by heart his incantations and genealogies and itineraries, to the Babylonian monarch who in his capacity of priest must have mastered the intricacies of astrology and the other established systems of divination, couched though they be in terms half-Sumerian, half-Semitic, and all more or less gibberish. Nor let it be forgotten that such sacred lore includes a knowledge not only of religious forms, but also of legal and judicial procedure, of which the whole operative value is held to lie in its being administered exactly. Thus in a way the social instinct of the ages before

civilization anticipates Plato's dream of the philosopher-king, who has been converted into a minister of
divine truth by means of an intensive education which
is likewise essentially a purgation.

But if philosophy in its political and moral aspects
has thus been ever closely associated with divinity,
what of science? Are not the natural sciences to be
regarded primarily as the outcome of various practical techniques, such as the smelting of metals, the
planting of crops, the healing of wounds, and so on?
No doubt they are; but this is not to say that magico-
religious influences have had nothing to do with the
development of the useful arts in question. In these
latter days, however, we are all too ready to oppose
science to superstition, as if whatever notions we now
class under the latter head had never had any historical connexion with the exploitation of the physical world, nay, with the very conception of Nature
as a superhuman dispenser of benefits. It must indeed
be admitted that scientific study has rid us of many a
false belief by insisting on fidelity to fact. On the
other hand, philosophers have always regarded the
dogmatic materialist as a half-educated person. Let
it be added, however, that their attitude towards the
physicist has of late become more sympathetic; for
the latter, thanks to his quantum theory and his doctrine of relativity, has become as it were despite himself a transcendentalist. Indeed, nowadays he is ready
to make common cause with art and religion in the
attempt to get into touch with a reality that, even in

its physical aspect, allows necessity no certain advantage over freedom.

To return to the savage, who has of course no conscious interest in such problems, he nevertheless has little use for what might be termed the subhuman categories, but on the contrary sees the miraculous and superhuman everywhere. As Lévy-Bruhl puts it, he is a mystic—that is, an indeterminist and an irrationalist, as we should express it in the language of modern thought—in all that regards the conduct of his life; so that in no sphere of it, not even the most familiar and workaday, is his preoccupation with the suprasensible for one moment relaxed. Hence his industrial pursuits are invariably akin to rituals. Their leading motive is to control the luck by a scrupulous attention to form. Occupational groups, therefore, tend to reproduce all the typical features of the secret society. Moreover, in proportion as a given craft is hereditary, the privacy that veils its methods is apt to be enhanced by association with the ancestral cult of some particular family or clan. Thus the mummeries and mystifications in which this primitive freemasonry is wont to revel—the cryptic signs, the enigmatic words, the ban of silence, and so forth— represent a stage of society when the language of the feelings is restricted to a crude symbolism, the outward expression of specialized knowledge and skill in alliance with a spirit of brotherhood and mutual aid. Before one rejoices that natural science has been purged of superstition, it may be therefore expedient

to look into the process whereby technical industry—
the parent source of natural science in so many of its
forms—has been purged of morality, and turned into
a wealth-seeking instead of a welfare-seeking process.
Already in the days of ancient Greece the forger of
the divine iron, Weyland Smith, had degenerated
into the *banausos,* the vile mechanic who toils by the
fire while gentlemen are disporting themselves afield.
Correspondingly there cannot but be something vile
and banausic about any purely mechanistic interpretation of the universe, the pragmatic effect of which
can only be to promote an industrialism equally soul-
less. Thus in proclaiming themselves to be mysteries,
the trade unions of the primitive world at least in-
vested their various callings with dignity. However
subconsciously, they stood for a kind of knowledge
and truth; and this, being associated with religion,
could not but maintain its affinities with morality, as
also with fine art. To a like extent, therefore, it was
safe against dehumanization—the fate attending all
theory or practice that subordinates the humanities to
physics, motives to bare causes.

It remains to speak of the charlatan—the man who
pretends to know, when he does not know. Naturally
such a type of knave is not peculiar to civilization.
Mr. Roth informs us, for example, how among the
aborigines of Queensland unlicensed practitioners of
medicine would sometimes impose on the public to
the scandal of the regular profession. Indeed it is
often maintained by shallow persons that all savages

are thorough humbugs, though more especially their chiefs and medicine-men. Much the same, however, is said about the leaders of modern society by those who, as Aristotle expresses it, get their view of the play from the cheap seats. In particular, some slip into the fallacy of deeming all religion more or less fraudulent because it employs a symbolism which, if taken literally, would be contrary to common sense. But this is to confuse the imaginative with the imaginary, the ideal with the merely unreal. Prefiguration is the only possible language of hope and faith; so that every true visionary, civilized or savage, takes liberties with the actual in order to provide the soul of his dream with some sort of picturable body. Now it may be that a power of intense and sustained vision —in a word, genius—is as rare in religion as in science, fine art, or any other branch of human activity. Be this as it may, genius is born rather than made; so that the object of any system of education must be chiefly to conserve and propagate its effects. This it does by training a body of experts—men who in default of genius at least have manifest talent; and their corporate efforts build up a tradition such as ensures the perpetuation of the creative influence. How many lost arts, as Dr. Rivers has shown, have savages had to deplore, owing simply to the precariousness of the means of transmission at a stage of society when continuous participation in a ritual is the only way of keeping truth alive? Let us not, then, undervalue the function under primitive conditions of those quasi-

professional fraternities which are the direct forerunners of our colleges and guilds. Their members
must not be set down as utter hypocrites if they make
up for a certain lack of inspiration by a meticulous
solicitude for external forms; not even if this inevitably carries with it a leaning towards shams. They
are the torch-bearers who pass along from hand to
hand the sacred fire kindled at divine altars. Without
such organs of transmission the higher education is
impossible.

The charlatan, then, must be sought outside the
ranks of the recognized groups that serve as ministers
of the social tradition. Thus at the level of savagery
the typical imposter is the dabbler in black magic,
because he is an individualist. I allow that it is often
a little hard to find any one precisely answering to
this description, at any rate in a healthy community
which stands no nonsense with those who practise on
the credulous for purely private ends. Nevertheless,
the wizard is not entirely a myth, but forms one of
those sporadic types which at every stage of society
provide a criminal element. Casually recruited and
continually harried as it is, such an underworld can
have no cohesion. Thus although some writers have
tried to prove that the alleged covens and sabbaths of
medieval witchcraft stood for secret organizations
that preserved essential features of pagan cult, it is
hard to believe that any genuine creed could survive
under such hole-and-corner conditions. On the contrary, one may declare on the strength of a far wider

induction than is supplied by Europe alone that the black or anti-social branch of occultism, to which the name of magic should be confined, has at no time any settled doctrine or meaning behind it; but is a jumble of mock rites, cribbed from the established religion of the day, and altogether caricatured and perverted in the process. The sorcerer, then, is a charlatan because he has served no apprenticeship in knowledge; the quality of the knowledge being always relative to the moral condition of the recipient soul. His dupes, too, are such base folk as have never known serious study or training in any form. Wherefore they remain at the mercy of appearances. They are incurious of truth, curious of gossip and idle tales. Hence when a false fear shakes them to pieces, they have no firm and tested belief on which to rally the disintegrated forces of the mind.

In conclusion, let us ask whether these historical considerations throw any light on the ideal relation of religion to science. Now it would seem that religion has done good service to the will to know by sanctifying the process of education, associating it with solemn and impressive forms, and likewise imparting a sense of brotherhood in those who participate in its mysteries. On the other hand, it might plausibly be maintained that education as promoted by religion has all along taken the humanities very seriously, and cosmology somewhat lightly. But, if in truth it shuns the domination of the lower or physical categories, this attitude is surely to be justified on the ground that the training of human character is of more vital importance than the improvement of our control over matter. So far, then, religion has reason to insist that natural science is inferior to moral philosophy in educative value. But science in its turn has a right to protest against the kind of supernaturalism that ignores the laws of evidence in its insistence on signs and wonders. Seeing how the sorcerer makes play with the monstrous for his pernicious ends, it is clear that it is part of the mission of science to liberate man from unworthy fears such as the terrorist is ever prone to exploit. In any case, truth of fact, though only one kind of truth, must be held by science and by religion in equal respect. It is only, however, when the pursuit of such truth inspires a life otherwise full of beauty and moral goodness that science rises to the level of a religion; and it is certain that such a pathway to religion proves the most accessible and attractive to many of the noblest spirits of our time.

IX

ADMIRATION

Religion is found in association with the desire to express beauty of form from the days of the cave-artists who, in the case of the animals represented, preserve a naturalistic style, though their masked human figures verge on the monstrous, as if the bestial still competed with the human in mystic value. Though stylized or purely geometrical art favours abstract thinking, emotion attaches more readily to concrete wholes, and in many ways fine art can assist religion in bringing out the quality of that which is worthy to be admired and loved.

As science has its emotional source in curiosity, so fine art can be said to arise out of admiration; although it may be well to remind ourselves at the start that, no less than science, fine art is an activity which, as such, involves a good deal more than simple feeling in its psychological composition. Considering them, however, simply from the side of the emotions, as it is our prime concern to do here, we note at once that the two have something in common; for both are disinterested attitudes of mind. It is, in fact, as if science and fine art alike invited a man to lose himself in the contemplation of the object. On the other hand, the relation with the object thus set up in each case is to all appearances different. The scientific interest is prying and penetrating. The artistic interest, in sharp contrast, would seem to be content with a surface-view. Thus the poet's passionate affirmation that 'beauty is truth, truth beauty' is, on the face of it, a paradox. Appearances are notoriously deceitful; so that the most artful rearrangement could scarcely remedy their natural illusoriness, but on the contrary might rather be rated as an additional falsification of the already false. If, then, the only approach to truth and reality were by the way of science, it might be hard to shake Plato's uncompromising verdict, namely, that an art such as poetry is something pleasant rather than conducive to the good life. It is only fair to add that Plato said this in the course of a polemic, directed no doubt chiefly against contemporary developments of the cheaper sort.

Nevertheless, William James was surely right when he bid us distinguish between 'knowledge of' and 'acquaintance with'—in other words, between piecemeal apprehension and wholesale comprehension. For wisdom is justified of both of these her children. Analysis and synthesis may, as some philosophers imagine, meet and merge in the Absolute. For human beings, however, who are still in process of learning, and hence can at best hope to become relatively wise, each method is bound to have the advantage over the other by turns. Aesthetic experience, therefore, is not to be disparaged offhand as a

way of truth because it makes no pretence to wield
the dissecting-knife of science, and hence is not pene-
trative in this almost literal sense. For let us recur
to the fact that in their full nature both science and
fine art are activities. This means that in our dealings with the world of things the initiative lies with
us; although in each case our emotional reaction to
the object involves a sort of self-surrender, as if we
allowed it to possess us, yet we ourselves started the
wooing. The mind is a Pygmalion who must create
his bride before she can come to life in his arms.
Now aesthetic experience of the artistic order is in
its mode of objectification synthetic rather than
analytic; and, in general, synthesis is prior to analysis
in the process of object-making. Out of the welter
of fleeting impressions something must be caught and
held; and this is done in the first instance by shaping
it—giving it form. For things to appear at all, they
must be seen at least in silhouette. Thus recognition
of the form will necessarily precede any exploration
of the matter. Before the parts can be examined
separately there must have been a preperception of
the whole. It would seem, then, that a sense of form is
the beginning of wisdom; and, since this can be also
said, though in a deeper sense, of the fear of God, it
may be that something can be done to bring these two
statements into line by studying fine art and religion
in their earliest historical relations with one another.

Now admiration is more than selective interest.
It might be defined as selective interest quickened by

love. In the struggle for existence man has to attend
to matters unpleasant as well as pleasant, and, maybe,
chiefly to the former. Even so, as R. L. Stevenson
tells the children,

> The world is so full of a number of things,
> I'm sure we should all be as happy as kings.

We can love the world, in our gregarious fashion,
for its very crowdedness. We enjoy gazing on the
many faces—at all events so long as they are friendly
faces. Unfortunately, however, the world is likewise
thronged with various sworn foes of our race whose
faces are intuitively odious; and to these we would
gladly shut our eyes, were it not necessary to be ever
watchful. At most we can snatch a timorous joy by
contemplating such forms of evil indirectly by means
of the imagination—as if one sat safely by the hearth
and saw bogey shapes in the fire. I am thinking of
the predilection sometimes evinced by religion for
the ugly and sinister in its acknowledged symbols.
Yet I am convinced that there is more hope than fear
at the heart of human religion. Hence the art that it
favours ought to rejoice chiefly in those lovable and
friendly forms of which there is so plentiful a supply
in Nature—she who is *daedala rerum,* 'fashioner of
things in their variety', as Lucretius, anticipating
Stevenson's thought, said long ago.

Admiration, however, does not in itself amount to
fine art, which is, so to say admiration become ex-
pressive instead of merely appreciative. Expression

implies the use of a medium or vehicle which is artificial in the sense that it is new matter adapted to
some lovable form in order the more clearly to bring
out its intrinsic charm, the grace inherent in its formal quality. Paradoxical as it may sound, the artist
transfers the matter to the form, not the form to the
matter; for we adapt the means to the end, and the
form whether it be given in nature or in idea is always
the final cause of the activity. This adaptation and
transference of the matter to suit the form must be
carried out adequately; and the skill shown in the
preparation of the medium of expression is what we
know as style. Thus style is not a primary, but a secondary or incidental, end of fine art; for, though it
stands to reason that, if there is to be expression of
the form, a certain measure of expressiveness must
be imparted to the vehicle, the latter result is attained
by the way. Hence to look no further than the style,
forgetting that it is but the minister of the form, is
a short-sighted policy bound to lead to disaster.
Stylism is the bane of art. It comes about chiefly
when artists seek to outdo one another instead of
seeking after the intrinsic beauty of the form which
can never be outdone. Thus the true artist must ever
concentrate on the form, and leave the style to look
after itself. Great art has an air of innocence and
freedom because it is on the face of it careless of
style. It always looks as if the genius had never
heard of art for art's sake.

How, then, can fine art and religion obtain mutual

benefit by association with each other? Possibly as follows. Religion can help fine art to realize that the form is of God, whereas the style is merely of the copyist Man. On the other hand, fine art can help religion to recognize the formal beauty of the archetypes provided by *Deus sive Natura*. Whether these things are so, however, cannot be discussed here thoroughly, but only in the light of certain early half-obliterated chapters of human history.

Plunge straight into the prehistoric, and what do we perceive? Fine art triumphant, and that almost at the very dawn of culture, as if the brightness of the coming day were already revealed in promise. Let us pass rapidly by the Mousterian and preceding periods that have left us little except their work in stone. Even here there is plenty to admire; and one regrets the loss of the woodwork, which, in hands that had obtained so complete a mastery over the harder material, must have lent itself to far more varied and delicate refinements. Neanderthal man may have had a brutish appearance, but one is inclined to say 'handsome is who handsome does', when one unearths in some cave-shelter, where also lie his bones, a very masterpiece of his making—a double-scraper, let us say, with finely retouched edges that from the trimmed butt or handhold spring symmetrically outwards and then gently recurve to a point, the whole implement not only shapely but glistening with natural colour. That we have nascent fine art here is more than likely. We may even expect a connexion with religion, seeing that the deposition of well-worked flints in graves—one actually lay by the hand of the Le Moustier skeleton and was, moreover, of unusual pattern—might seem to imply a ceremonial use. It would, however, be useless to speculate how far this would affect the status and outlook of the artist—whether it would involve him in a special initiation and special taboos, and in short would turn him into the high-priest of a mystery, whose work was full of wonder for all, because all saw it as part of a greater wonder.

We are on firmer ground when we pass on to those later phases of the Palaeolithic epoch which are marked in Europe by the advent of *Homo sapiens*—our modest way of describing the man of our own type. Our progenitor, as one might almost call him, and certainly our cousin at a good many removes, has left us memorials of his artistic taste and skill that definitely place his work on a par with the choicest output of subsequent ages. Art is very loosely attached to the time-process, just as a beautiful flower may appear at almost any season. Homer sang divinely when most of 'the glory that was Greece' was yet to be; and in like manner painters and carvers whose names we can never know wrought divinely when all the civilization of Europe could so far be contained within a cave. Before glacial times were well over, they sprang up like snowdrops. Whereas, however, the historian can gratefully record the fact, he is at his wits' end to find any

the painting to the irregularities of the surface; for all along any hint of meaning in the shape of the cave-wall is dutifully noted and developed by the painter, as well might be the case if the cave itself were sacred.

Before leaving the Magdalenian artists we might pause a moment to consider why they concentrate on animal forms and on the whole show little interest in the human figure. Is it sheer neglect, or deliberate avoidance dictated by the fear of magic? Surely some taboo on depicting human beings, or at any rate the male of the species, in too realistic a shape must have prevailed in the Franco-Cantabrian region; seeing how away in Eastern Spain more or less contemporary Capsians could indulge freely in a scenography of their daily life such as often verges on light *genre*. In the north, however, one suspects that religion tolerated only the representation of the sacred form of the masked dancer. The so-called 'sorcerer' of the cave of Les Trois Frères, with the head of a reindeer and the limbs of a man, is the outstanding example of this style. Was it good taste, or simple accident, which withheld Magdalenian art from developing in such a direction; for that way lies the monstrous? Between a pure theriomorphism and a pure anthropomorphism there can be no compromise that does not jar on the senses. No doubt religion has to be forgiven if it sees fit to employ composite symbols; for a juxtaposition of incompatible images is by no means fatal to a consistent

conception of the divine any more than a mixture of
metaphors need destroy the meaning of a sentence.
Nevertheless, neither literature nor any other kind of
art is served by the contamination and confusion of
what might be called the archetypes of creation.
What Nature has put asunder, let no man join.
Goethe has said that the true artist is he who can
work within limits; and here is a limit beyond which
aesthetic propriety should never dare to go. Fine
art, in a word, abhors the abnormal. Satyrs, centaurs,
and even mermaids cannot rise far above the gro-
tesque; while the androgynous is always allied to the
obscene. Beauty is neither for the frivolous nor the
unchaste, but is the reward of a certain sanity of
soul, which disciplines the imagination so that it
observes the mean, and hence rejects the monstrous
in all its forms.

Not for a moment, however, would I be supposed
to condemn the Magdalenians for their masked
dancer, though I congratulate them on having by
choice or by chance abstained from seeking therein
a leading motive for their graphic art. After all, if
there ever was a time when the human could in all
seriousness represent itself as the semi-bestial it was
in days when it had barely thrust up its head above
the dead level of surrounding animality. Thus those
proto-Darwinians, the Arunta of Central Australia,
have hardly yet made up their minds whether their
ancestors were men or marsupials; and so, too, the
European cave-man some ten or fifteen thousand

years earlier may have been similarly prone to iden-
tify himself with the cave-bear, and his next-door
neighbour with the cave-hyena. So long, then, as
mankind conceived its relationship to the beasts in
terms of alliance rather than of mastery and over-
lordship—the latter stage following only on their
domestication—religion, ever tolerant of mystery,
might well hesitate whether to look forwards or
backwards; although fine art, trusting to its instinct
for beauty, had already committed itself to the
idealization of the distinctively human. For the
Arunta commemorate their totemic descent—by no
means clearly envisaged as an ascent—in heroic
drama involving the use of stage-properties copied,
or literally borrowed, from animals and even plants.
Yet, even so, the soul of the play resides in the human
acting; not to speak of the human authorship behind
the acting, which is so well recognized an element in
the technique that a sort of copyright law has already come into operation. So far, then, as these
performances amount to art—and they no doubt have
likewise some religious value for the Arunta, though
no explanation of what it may be has hitherto been
extracted from them—their form is not essentially
determined by their theriomorphic adjuncts. Much
later, when Greek drama piously retains the mask,
it can have got little good from it; except, perhaps,
in comedy, where the antic touch is permissible—the
sort of frolicsome by-play that leads an Arunta
dancer to imitate the silly movements of an emu's

head, so as to raise a laugh in the crowd. In general, however, the course of development pursued by the most serious and significant forms of the dramatic art have led it further and further away from masquerading and mummery of all kinds.

To revert to the subject of the monstrous, it must be noted that, though never beautiful, it can be deeply impressive, and perhaps for better as well as for worse. Certainly religious symbolism, at the stage at which it still mostly depends for its appeal to the mind on visible and concrete forms, shows no compunction in outraging the decencies of sense with its maladaptions to the human form of the head of a foul-feeding bird of prey, the many arms of a spider, or the many dugs of a sow. If it is revolting as art, it may be edifying as allegory, and one must leave it at that. But the candid historian of human religion must not make the mistake of regarding all its manifestations as equally healthy—that is, equally consonant with its true mission to mankind. A major fallacy to which it has always been liable is to confound the supernatural with the unnatural. But there is a world of difference between the ideal and the abnormal. The latter being out of measure is at once artistically and morally wrong. In order to conceive the divine, religion can but endeavour to assemble all the measures and norms of perfection revealed in our imperfect human nature; but to negate the human by substituting the bestial is, instead of cleansing the soul of its incrustations, to thrust it back further than ever into the slime. Not that we need be puritanically severe in our insistence on a complete break with traditional forms that err against this canon. By all means let the Devil retain his horns and hoofs; for they are appropriate. As for angels, they may have their wings as long as they stand in them and do not use them in flight; since I never saw a pictured angel yet that flew anything but heavily. Nevertheless, let monsters as a class be consigned to the religions of fear; and these, I believe, are aberrations through and through. Speaking for myself, at any rate, I can only shudder, not with *horror religiosus* but with downright disgust, at the portentous shapes associated with blood-stained rites in West Africa, Ancient Mexico, or even more civilized India. These are on the face of them abominable things—perversities. The art enslaved to such a devil-worship is in itself devilish, whatever technical excellence it may have in the eyes of those who cannot realize that style and significance are óne.

It remains to consider the more abstract kind of symbolism which is also germane to religious art. I see no reason to think that a design approaching to the geometrical is invariably a degraded holomorph; though undoubtedly the substitution of part for whole has had its share in producing the ideogram. For it seems quite possible that an arrangement of notches, made, let us say, in the course of whittling a stick with a flintknife should please the eye by its symmetry, and should on future occasions be reproduced for the sake of the decorative effect. Such notching might, moreover, have meanwhile acquired another sort of meaning as a *memoria technica* serving for tally or message-stick. In certain cases, then, one might expect the aesthetic and the semantic interests to combine—just as they do in precious manuscripts or incunabula of which the form is worthy of the contents. Thus a formalism almost entirely of the mind's making, as being derived from artificial characters bearing little or no sensible likeness to the things for which they stand, may come into existence side by side with the naturalism that recalls things in and by their concrete appearance. Between these opposite poles of art all manner of intermediate styles are found; but, in proportion as mental evolution favours intelligence of the logical and mathematical type, all the gain is likely to be on the side of formalism and the loss on the other. Representationism, with its naïve desire to tell a story, goes down before the symbolism that is content to indicate a thought by means of a cipher. Truth who once wore a garment of many colours down to her feet has had it gradually curtailed by her advisers until to-day there is often nothing left but a few threads.

Now were religion of the pure intellect rather than of the heart, that central organ to which intellect and even consciousness itself are subject, all might be well, and a symbolism of the most formal type might suffice for its needs. But religion is a

matter of full-blooded emotion, and therefore cannot afford to cut itself off from the sense-channels
that feed the nobler feelings such as admiration.
Nay, its best method of eliminating the sensual is
to give the sensuous full power to enrich and gladden
the serious life. At most then the grosser forms of
sense-symbolism must be gradually discarded. The
old-world celebrations involving unbounded eating
and drinking can be spiritualized until completely
purged of their licence. Then, as regards smell, the
odour of sanctity need not be reinforced by artifice,
not even by means so seductive as the use of tobacco.
As for complicated vestments and the like, if they
go the way of masks, they may not greatly be missed
any more than the garish uniforms of the obsolete
type of soldier. But these things hardly come within
the domain of the fine arts. Architecture, however,
does; for, though its material is gross, it handles it
finely, impressing the delicate texture of a dream on
the crude timber and stone and baked mud. Nay,
architecture might almost be said to come into being
under the inspiration of religion; for the idea of a
God's house awoke the imagination of the builder as
that of a man's house had never done before. May it
be long before a country is prouder of its railway-
stations and banks than of its temples! Of painting
and sculpture enough, perhaps, has been already
said. Suffice it to add that, although secular influences have encouraged much good work, it has, perhaps, always needed the impulsion of religion to

attain the sublime; witness Phidias as against Praxi-
teles, or Raphael as against Rubens. There remains
the symbolism of sounds as embodied in literature
and music. Whereas its secular literature is the glory
of the West, the aesthetic quality of its religious writ-
ings is not so well sustained, nor is this on a par with
the inspiration of the Ancient East, unless the Vedas,
the Psalms, and the Book of Job are judged to be
sufficiently offset by Plato, Dante, and Milton.
Music, however, which touches the heights at least
as often in its religious as in its lay efforts, is essentially European and modern; and it may be that a
symbolism so ethereal in its sense-mechanism and
hence so well fitted to express intellectual beauty will
prove most satisfying to the religion of the future.

And what of the present? Any study of the savage
is bound to yield this reflection: that, if he is too
undifferentiated in his way of life, we on our part
may be over-specialized in ours. Plenty of factory-
hands are available, but there seem to be altogether
too few wise heads in charge of the business of living
well. Now it is plainly the function of religion to
play the Platonic philosopher-king and rule in the
name of the Good; but how are the disunited
churches going to unify the world? Perhaps they
would be more likely to forget their dissensions if
they thought more of their common task, which is to
make mankind one in heart and soul. Perhaps, too,
the way to set about it would be to make more of
beauty as an aid to good living. If a love of beauty

came out so early in our race, it must lie pretty deep. Nothing, however, can stir the depths of the inner man so effectually as religion; though history shows that, by doing so, it brings up to the surface good and bad alike. But beauty is the least ambiguous of all the good things of life. So here at least is a sound doctrine for religion to preach—that more beauty means more love.

X

CHARITY

Prehistoric times were no golden age in which peace and charity reigned throughout the earth, but within the primitive home the woman must have played her natural part of peacemaker; while her curse may well have been the primal sanction against the shedding of kinly blood, even if her lamentations did much to stimulate blood-revenge. So, too, endo-cannibalism, cutting for the dead, and blood-brotherhood are rites making for consciousness of kind. As contrasted with a just but heartless legalism, charity gives freely without insisting on reciprocity.

A CONCLUDING lecture must somehow conclude; and an argument which reserves its last word for the subject of charity can surely claim to be received in a like spirit. Not that civilized folk must suppose themselves to have a monopoly of that crowning virtue. The primitive world is less uncharitable than is sometimes believed. Our present object, however, is not to evaluate savage charity considered in itself, but rather to observe how its quality is affected by its historical connexion with religion. Now we who profess a religion of charity might be tempted to assume offhand that only good could result from

such an association. But history is more concerned
with deeds than with professions; nor does Chris-
tianity provide the only type of human religion.
Actually the religious record displays a chequered
pattern of white and black; and the clue to this unedi-
fying fact is to be found in the ambivalence of religious emotion. After all, the touch-stone of charity
lies in the question: 'Is it peace or war, O my neighbour?' Now the natural man will sometimes fight
like a tiger. But the religious man is apt to fight like
a fiend.

In old days the problem whether the state of nature, that is, the pre-civil condition of mankind, was
a state of universal war or of universal peace would
provoke hot debate among the philosophers.
Hobbes says one thing, Rousseau the opposite; while
Locke, less given to rhetoric than either of the others,
is inclined to compromise, but on the whole gives a
lead to Rousseau. When more modern thinkers, with
better information at their disposal, offer to pronounce on a point so nearly touching the honour of
our race, they are prone to be tendencious, and so
remain unconvincing. Their one-sidedness provokes
the suspicion that this writer is at heart a pacifist, and
that one an upholder of the supremacy of the big
blonde beast. For the impartial verdict of history
is, surely, that human nature is neither good nor bad
but mixed; and the same estimate holds of every
activity that issues forth from that common matrix
of mingled clay and flame. Pre-eminently, then, does

it apply to religion, which of all our activities is by far the most central and comprehensive.

I would ask you, then, to imagine Neanderthal man in his cave-home. His temper may have been uncertain, and he may have snarled even over his supper. Yet he was doubtless loyal enough to his own folk; who, when they were full of the meat that he had brought in, snuggled together not ungratefully by the fire that he knew how to kindle and keep alive. As for the rest of his kind, he would probably not like the smell of them, and would duly flourish his club at them and show his canines. But was he much troubled with neighbours? Europe must have been very thinly populated in those days, to judge by the distribution and contents of the known Mousterian sites; and one may suspect that a living specimen of *Homo primigenius* was nearly as rare a spectacle along the banks of the ancient Thames or Somme as nowadays is a gorilla amid the forests of the Congo. On the other hand, in Upper Palaeolithic times there was more society for those who could appreciate it. One cannot be sure, of course, that the shelters which honeycomb the valley-walls of the Vézère in Dordogne were occupied contemporaneously; but so many burrows seem to imply a warren, and the chances are that, like the Eskimo, these later cave-men were well on their way to become villagers and almost townsfolk. Such close aggregation may, of course, have been seasonal; the people scattering for the summer hunting and, when the cold came on, re-

assembling to eat down their hoards, as also to hold
ceremonies to bring back better weather and more
game. Yet, continuous or not, it was a wider and
richer social life, a notable enlargement of the original fire-circle.

Even so, all was not peace, if one can read the signs
aright. True, along the Vézère nothing survives to
suggest fighting, unless it be a suspicious hole in a
Cro-Magnon lady's head—a mere by-product, I dare
say, of divorce proceedings, or of funeral custom.
Further South, however, the Capsians have left us
battle-pictures full of spirit. There cannot, indeed,
be the least doubt about the whole-heartedness with
which they shoot arrows into one another from bows
of formidable size until, at any rate as the artist
would have us believe, the victims are more like por-
cupines than men. These same Capsians were probably intruders from Africa; so that a defender of
the priority of amity to enmity might be disposed to
belittle war as a secondary effect of immigration.
Yet, however far we go back in human history, we
must constantly postulate, and can often prove, mi-
gration. But how gratuitous would be the assumption that new settlers invariably found bare lots to
occupy without dispute; seeing that early movements
of peoples are confined to natural corridors where
constriction immediately leads to crowding. Add
that, as far as pre-history can take us, man is already
a meat-eater and a killer—one, moreover, who is
capable of standing up to fierce beasts which, as com-

pared with his fellow men, were, if not so subtle-brained, at least more heavily armed. Or, again, in reply to the argument that war involves organization and must therefore have evolved late, it can be urged that hunting too involves organization. Nay, the very shortcomings of the primitive hunter's armament made it all the more imperative that he should imitate the methods of the wolf-pack. That rival hordes of men would never clash and have it out is too much to believe, if, restraining sentiment, one gives the probable facts their due weight. If, then, the pacifist cannot extract the admission that he wants out of pre-history, he has lost his case; for history is a witness on the other side. The evidence concerning the civilized peoples with literary records shows decisively that they come from fighting stocks, and that the non-combatant elements, if any, have enjoyed none of the prevailing culture except the scraps. Such, then, is human nature seen in retrospect. Yet that it can be improved by education, until charity comes finally to her own, is at least the hope of the future. For charity is home-worthiness. If men could be made to feel and behave as if they were at home in the wide world and in the universe, they would not want to fight any longer; for fighting in the home has been a great taboo, as far as ever human history goes back.

Now it is historically as well as otherwise true that charity begins at home. As an historical statement, however, this needs to be justified by adding that the primitive home in its earliest forms is more or less uni-parental. The typical savage belongs either to his mother's or to his father's people, and, one may be pretty sure, originally to his mother's. Parental instinct in the female is a more straightforward affair than in the male, and, biologically speaking, the family is older than religion. For the degree of its evolution may be roughly measured by the retardation that has taken place in the attainment of puberty; and this with human beings is a lengthy process involving a fosterage equally protracted. Instinct, however, merely preforms intelligence. It but furnishes a rough scheme on which man's conscious experience gradually refines and improves. Mother-right, then, in the extremest forms known to us has become a moral institution. At the same time we find it already permeated with religious feeling, which on the whole raises the significance to a higher level, though in its ambivalent way it provokes extravagances as well as exaltations. Thus the mother, who is essential woman, is at once holy and unclean. Much that need not be repeated here has been written about the disabilities incurred by her for no better reason than that all saw in her the proximate and, as they long thought, the sole source of family as identified with the blood-tie. But the complementary fact has been somewhat overlooked, namely, that, being pre-eminently taboo and having *mana* in like proportion, she was in a strong position to exert a will of her own; and I believe that the will of the essential woman is for peace in the home, and that is to say for charity.

Thus, in native Australia it is always the woman who plays the peace-maker. When rival bucks are at loggerheads, she rushes in between them and they stop—for no dog bites the lady-dog—and besides, since bravery is first-cousin to bluff, it may be that secretly they are only too glad to do so. Further, when different groups ingeminate war to the last flint-knife, off go the women as ambassadors to patch up the squabble; and even that rude chivalry respects their sacrosanct character. How much more, then, must the Mother be potent for peace within her own fire-circle! To disobey her is to feel accursed; for by right of her position she is high-priestess of the religion and laws of the blood. Now it was suggested in a previous lecture that, away back in the beyond of history, she may have initiated exogamy by insisting on chaste relations among camp-mates, partly from a nascent sense of the decencies of life, but partly also and perhaps chiefly in order to suppress murderous jealousies at all costs. Be this as it may, we have no knowledge of the time when it was not a bed-rock principle of human society that the blood of the brotherhood is sacred and must not be shed; and that brotherhoods are but enlarged motherhoods is at least more likely than not. So unthinkable, indeed, is such a sin, that primitive law rarely makes provision for dealing with it. Indeed, the fear of thus rendering oneself abominable and outcast be-

yond all redemption is sufficient sanction to keep the
passions of the wildest savage in check. Call it
instinct—the law of the wolf-pack—and you most
certainly are under the mark. Not to mention the
fact that parental care would seem to be much more
strongly developed in our race than any gregarious
tendency that it may likewise possess, the very invio-
lability of the law against shedding kinly blood pro-
claims it a taboo—an organized curse; and I believe
that there is a mother's curse at the back of it. For
whose blood is it that cries out for divine vengeance
if it is not ultimately hers?

But if it is only intestine and so to speak consan-
guine murder that provokes the divine vengeance of
the Furies—those Erinyes whom more than once
Homer definitely identifies with a mother's curses—
what of the murder done by a stranger which almost
as automatically incurs human vengeance in the
shape of retaliation by the kin? For the three fundamental laws of blood-fellowship are these: no incest;
no internal bloodshed; and blood for blood against
the rest of the world. Nor is this third law much less
binding, if at all, than the other two. The nearest
thing to conscience exhibited by an Australian native
is, perhaps, the sense of dissatisfaction at a good deed
left undone which comes over him if he has been
somehow prevented from avenging a kinsman's
death; and that though he blindly imputes the disaster to the evil magic of alien persons unknown. It
certainly is no mere blood-lust that inspires him; but

a righteous indignation prompting him to a truly
religious duty. Who, then, was originally responsible
for the sacred obligation? Once more, I suggest that
it was the woman; even if by so doing I make it
appear that her charity not only begins at home but
ends there. I am not merely thinking of that most
repulsive plate in Spencer and Gillen which figures
the Illapurinja or avenging woman; who, despite
her sex, is allowed to carry a *churinga* as a badge
of her sacred office. I rely rather on the universal
law of human life that 'men must work and women
must weep'. It is always the latter who take the lead
in the frenzied lamentations so characteristic of the
funeral rites of the savage. No doubt custom has to
some extent formalized them; and yet for the fashion
to have arisen they must have come from the heart in
the first instance. Now in Australia it is a common
insult for one native to taunt another with not having
gashed himself for the dead as deeply as he might.
How much more effectively, then, if only because
they could not be answered with a blow, must the
women be able to pour scorn on the warriors who
could look upon their dead and let the matter rest—
for there could be no resting for the hapless dead if
they did. But even bravest Hector feared what the
Trojan women might say.

It would be impracticable here, though not irrele-
vant, to consider systematically the manifold features
of what might be termed the religion of the blood-
tie. Moreover, were it so possible we should have to

give the religious that wide connotation that equates it with the ceremonial in all its more serious aspects; for our present interest is in the emotional side of religion, and ceremony is its chosen instrument for kindling and propagating psychic infection in the crowd. Nay, we should be driven to explore the inward meaning of an entire stage of human society, namely, the totemistic; for the clan-totem is essentially a name signifying that the kinsfolk are, as the Australian native puts it, 'all-one-flesh'; flesh, blood, *mana,* and soul being but successive refinements of the same sentiment and idea. Thus to the anthropologist endo-cannibalism is not simply disgusting, because he can perceive the underlying principle of kindly feeling that seeks expression in this crude act of communion. To participate in the virtues of the departed hero, and to neutralize the aggressive disposition of a ghost loth to go off by himself, are, I think, but secondary interpretations springing from the root-notion that to eat of the dead is to eat with them. Or, again, the rite of cutting for the dead, which in itself might seem to be meant entirely for their benefit—and undoubtedly the motive of revitalizing the corpse by sprinkling it literally or metaphorically with the blood of the mourners is a real one, being borne out by the custom of administering youthful blood to the old and feeble—is but a special form of a wider practice of blood-exchange. Witness the fact that, if an Australian youth opens his veins for the sake of a decrepid elder, the latter in his prime had already done the same for many a novice at initiation, baptizing him so copiously with the mystic water of life that the donor was ready to faint before he thought of desisting. Not to dwell further on old-world ceremonies, for a close examination of which our nerves are too delicate—or, shall we say, not sufficiently robust?—blood-brotherhood is a custom with a distribution as wide as its significance is deep; the life-and-death attachment of an Orestes to a Pylades, or of David for Jonathan being its echo in sacred story. But blood-brotherhood and milk-brotherhood are ultimately one, even if blood prevails in ritual as the more procurable medium of expression. Aristotle in the *Politics* has not forgotten that clansmen are men of the same milk—'homogalacts'. Here, then, at least there can be nothing to offend our taste. Religious symbolism has said its last word when it conceives charity as the mother's milk of human kindness.

Now I have purposely dwelt, anthropologist fashion, on the far-off beginnings of things, and have done such prolonged obeisance before the shrine of the Mothers that it is high time to take some notice of fatherhood—after-thought though it would seem to have been in the social and mental history of our race. A father in the social sense of the term may be defined as a domesticated human male. Whether his domestication was anterior to that of the other useful animals is uncertain, though it is perhaps more certain that it has never been so complete. Woman may

have succeeded in taming the dog by petting him as
a puppy, to judge by the way the young dingo
responds to feminine endearments. But to tame the
husband vicariously by petting the pledges of their
mutual passions was a far less effective way of bringing the former into subjection. After all, he is first
and foremost his mother's son, and his wife is but the
daughter of his mother-in-law, of Her-who-must-
be-avoided. Starting thus as the furtive lover, such
affection as he might feel towards his wife—and
some tenderness might on biological analogy be expected to enter into even a cave-man's wooing—
would necessarily be of a sneaking kind. He has
little chance of cultivating it in her home where her
big brothers do their best to make him feel small and
out of it. Nay, his very children are more theirs than
his, and are hardly more disposed than their elders
to extend their charity towards him. Nor, when custom at length permits him to carry off the wife to
his own people, is it to a home of his own so much
as to his mother's home that she unwillingly is led.
We have only to think of the Bantu custom whereby
the mother and sisters of the husband ceremoniously
insult the new-come bride, partly to break her in, but
partly too, it would seem, to work off their natural
repressions. No doubt the change from matrilocal
to patrilocal marriage makes for male dominance
in the long run; but at first one uni-parental system has but given way to another, and the bi-parental
family is still a long way in the offing. The trans-

ported wife trails her kinship with her and breeds
little aliens in the camp of the stranger. Her husband has got her services but not her spiritual
allegiance. Conversely, she has no call or right to
mother him; and she teaches her children to be lov-
ing towards herself, but at most to fear and respect
their common lord and master.

Thoroughly unstable, however, is the compromise
between mother-right and father-right that occurs
when marriage is patrilocal but kinship remains
matrilineal. An allegiance divided between the moral
claims of scattered blood-mates and the physical
supremacy of the father as the man on the spot must
break down one way or the other, and in the long
run it is authority that prevails over sentiment. The
new order maintains a nominal continuity of principle with the old by identifying family as before
with the name. But the gentile patronymic could
never acquire the mystic significance of the name that
stood for mother's blood. Though it eventually took
over the entire stock of implications, exogamy, the
ban on mutual slaughter and the duty of communal
revenge, the emotional basis had shifted from a semi-
biological stir of the blood to a sociological convention. The change, like any other major process of
history, was perhaps inevitable and has certainly
proved irreversible. It paved the way towards ever
wider forms of social union, from *gens* to tribe and
eventually from city-state to nation. A stable legalism founded on paternal discipline once and for all

displaced the tumultuous régime of mother-love reinforced by the shrill sanction of mother-rage. But the new charity was, in Aristotle's phrase, watery; for, as water is to blood, so is any kind of law-made civism to a home-made consciousness of kin. Not until a long process of social evolution has established the bi-parental family by bringing about the legal and moral equality of husband and wife, does the home resume its archetypal function as a nursery of the gentler feelings. A one-sided patriarchalism is always harsh—even in its religion, which, being typically a manes-worship, imputes a father's imperiousness to the forefathers, and figures them with ghostly rods in their hands. The Bantu expects his ancestors to fight on his side; but he likewise regards their arbitrary and so to speak freakish chastisements as the cause of half his troubles. The Roman observes the sacred rites of the *gens* with cold correctness, and thinks possessively not only of the wife who, as his law puts it, is fast in his hand, but even in regard to his Lares and Penates who are essentially guardians of his property. But perhaps it is to China that we must look for the apotheosis of the patriarchal idea. Of course in an area of such dense population the gentile organization has gone. By a remarkable survival, however, it is still prohibited to marry within the patronymic; and yet there are only some four hundred of these surnames to be shared among almost as many millions of souls. But though the individual family has thus become the social unit, and though an intensive cult of ancestors might almost be said to have given it the status of a religious order, it immobilizes and interns the woman; and, presumably for this reason, becomes the school of a morality that is ceremonious, intellectual, and rather heartless. In short, too much insistence on father-right may account for the arrested development to be perceived not only in China but to some extent also in the pagan world of the Greeks and Romans; for in both cases their entire philosophy of life looks no further than to a tranquillity of the mind, while a charity of the soul remains beyond its horizon.

It is, unfortunately, not possible here to examine in full detail the ethics of the early home as it warmly gathers round the hearth of charity, that is to say, the mothering principle. Perhaps enough has been said to illustrate its negative and disciplinary side which is summed up in the precept: 'Let us not quarrel among ourselves.' It has been shown how not only the taboo on intestine homicide, but even the exogamic law that fighting about women is indecent except outside, may be regarded as special applications of this rule. It only remains to add in this context that the prohibition against internal bickering is so obviously salutary that society in its later and wider developments never goes back on the injunction. One has only to think of the serious view which is always and everywhere taken of slander. Burmese law, for instance, is said to recognize and

punish twenty-seven distinct kinds. Nay, just because in primitive times the rest of the world is conceived as hostile, it is plain to all that there is no
room for hostility within the limits of natal and
tribal association. Thus Powers tells of the Pomo of
California that they had two chiefs, a war-chief and
a peace-chief. The latter must be some wise old man
who had done with war, and his function was to
adjust disputes and to keep angry passions, and in
particular sexual jealousy, within strict bounds.
Moreover, on this point religion is in entire sympathy with law. For instance, Miss Fletcher in her
interesting account of the Sioux ghost-lodge explains
how necessary it is to abstain from quarrels in its
vicinity—or, as an Ancient Roman would say, *favere
linguis;* among other reasons because ghosts have a
delicate constitution and hate any disturbance of
the air.

But the primitive ethics of charity may also be
said to have a positive side, of which the purport is
contained in the broad commandment: 'Give freely.'
In the cave-home this must virtually have meant the
same thing as 'Eat fair'. The Arunta rubs his stomach with a sacred stone in order to soften his feelings
and make him more generous in the distribution of
food. Such a fact indicates that the extreme gener-
osity displayed, as all observers testify, by the savage
hunter in this respect is not entirely spontaneous, but
is a product of management—doubtless such management as a mother has still occasionally to exercise

in the course of a nursery tea. Here or hereabouts, then, is to be sought the secret of that give-and-take which is so marked a feature of the simpler type of human society. It can almost be said to know no other law of property than 'Share and share alike'. Now we confirmed individualists are only too ready to insist that such a sentiment can be carried too far. When Darwin's Fuegian friend Jimmy Button tore all his European clothes to rags in order that his friends might participate in his finery, he offered up the decencies of civilization on the altar of a pre-sartorial morality. Such undiscriminating liberality undoubtedly does not make for that independence of effort which is needed for an age of competition. For the Samoan, Turner writes: 'The entire tribe or clan was his bank.' Is it not more than a coincidence if the Samoan ranks low among the world's workers? Yet this is to look at the matter from a European point of view; such as is only too apt to overlook the altogether festive delight with which the same Samoan enters into the communal job of setting up a house or hollowing out a canoe. It is, in short, anachronistic to estimate the pros and cons of primitive collectivism—it is hardly a communism—from the standpoint of an advanced ethics. This is based largely on the idea of justice, and is suitable for widespread communities that actually are held together less by love than by economic advantage. Quite otherwise is it with the mothering principle, which makes little or no distinction between the useful and the useless units of the brood, being rather by ancient instinct impelled to be patient with the helpless. Far more than justice, or even equity, charity is long-suffering. It is emotional rather than rational, feminine rather than male, because it hopes against hope and is reckless of results. Charity is the pelican who feeds her young from her own vitals and gives without return. Thus charity is more than liberality. The self-display of the profuse is recompensed with honour at the least, while the giver of a *potlatch* even expects to be repaid in kind and in effect is but putting out his money at interest. But charity, which is not of the head but of the heart, or, one might even say, of the womb, has no gain in prospect unless it be the good of the race; and this is felt immanently here and now, rather than projected by thought on to the mists of the future.

It remains to connect charity with self-sacrifice, if it can be done without forcing the historical facts. We have seen that it may well have been woman, always so prone to indulge in the luxury of grief, who initiated the practice of cutting for the dead. The institution of sacrifice has many roots, but this is one of them. Even if we prefer to regard suttee as rather a tragedy of patriarchalism, a sort of suicide on the part of the widow left desolate among strangers and with no better alternative than to be handed over to her husband's brother, we have evidence in the self-scarifications and self-mutilations of very primitive folk such as the Australians that religious

custom seized on these moments of emotional abandon to formalize them as part of a fixed tribute paid
to the memory of their dead. Now that the woman
should give her blood for the sake of the living is
nature's law; but that she should give it on behalf
of a corpse gone for ever cold is, biologically speaking, a sheer aberration. It is waste, in any but a religious sense, to gash oneself over a grave; just as it is
waste on a larger scale to shoot a hundred and fifty
horses—as was done at the funeral of a Blackfoot
chief—or to destroy even larger numbers of human
beings in one fell slaughter, as used to happen in
Tropical Africa when the last honours were paid to
some great king. Contemplating such unhappy
things the anthropologist is more ready to think of
cruelty—a subject with which we have already dealt
—than of fair charity in relation to the blood-sacrifice in any form; even if, thanks largely to the gift-
theory of sacrifice, its motive is gradually sublimated
until it is viewed as the oblation to God of a pure
heart. It seems better, then, to argue that it was not
of their charity that the mothers of the blood-kin cut
themselves for their lost brethren and sons, but rather
of their temporary despair—a morbid tendency from
which they were recalled by the need of giving their
wantonly lacerated breasts to their hungry offspring.
For if self-sacrifice looks away from the life of this
world, charity must ever look towards it, throwing
itself with no less abandon into the task of nursing
and educating it forward. It is no sacrifice of the

mother to suckle her child. Nay, it is the nearest thing to communion on God's earth, and may therefore stand as the perfect symbol of peaceful and bountiful love, as it might be not only in the Communion of Saints, but likewise among us poor human beings. Charity is no late message sent down to civilized folk from heaven. It is something that whispers in the very life-blood of the race; as if it were the tender voice of the Earth-mother bidding us remember that we are all her children.

INDEX

237